M L Harkey

PREACHING

CONFESSION

THE LORD'S SUPPER

Walter Lüthi
Eduard Thurneysen

PREACHING

CONFESSION

THE LORD'S SUPPER

Translated by Francis J. Brooke, III

JOHN KNOX PRESS
RICHMOND, VIRGINIA

Library of Congress Catalog Card Number: 60-9291

First published in 1957 by Evangelischer Verlag A. G., Zollikon-Zurich.

Printed in the United States of America

6061

CONTENTS

The Church of the Word

IN THE MARKET PLACE of a certain Swiss city a widely read daily newspaper maintains a show window where each day the latest news bulletins are posted. During the last war a large crowd had gathered there at noon one day when important news was expected from the front. The crowd began to push and shove, and there were shouts of impatience from those at the rear. Suddenly someone near the window climbed up on the ledge and in a loud voice began to read the news of what had happened.

At first glance, this event is not dissimilar to what customarily happens on Sunday mornings when someone from the flock enters the pulpit to read aloud what has taken place. As a rule, one person reads and interprets the Word, while the others listen. This one person usually stands somewhat above the others, although of course this does not mean that he stands nearer to God than the congregation of listeners. His elevated position is merely practical, and essentially without significance. It is also not important whether this encounter with the Word takes place in a regular church building, a schoolroom, a grain mill, or a hospital ward; it is only essential that there be reading and listening. The central element in the Protestant church service is the Word—preaching. "Who is going to hear the sermon tomorrow?" I have heard this Saturday question ever since my childhood, and it shows no signs of demise in the Protestant home. Sometimes the father, but more frequently the mother, asks the question after dinner, just as the table is being cleared. The Catholic Christian goes to church, but the Protestant hears the sermon.

Since the Reformation, Protestantism has justifiably called itself the "Church of the Word." But is it really? We have just said that the Protestant Christian goes to hear the sermon. But does he really go? Recently I met a woman who had left her church and joined a sect. A domestic servant by vocation and no longer a young woman, she is a Christian of some experience with life. This independent woman told me of her thirty-five years of service in the homes of farmers, artisans, businessmen, officials, and intellectuals—nine homes all told. Although she did not speak derogatorily about her former employers, she finally did mention what had disturbed her in each position: it was impossible for her to go to church on Sunday mornings. Her employers would sleep late on Sunday, not to refresh themselves after their week's work but to recuperate from their activities of Saturday night. She then had to prepare breakfast, straighten up the rooms, and cook dinner—all without a break. This mode of life she felt customary among us Protestants, and she went on to say that all of her employers were baptized Christians, the overwhelming majority being Protestants.

Martin Luther taught us to sing, "They must let the Word alone," and indeed we have let it alone, but not as the Reformer meant. To tell the truth, we have let it very much alone. Nonetheless, evangelical Christianity is the "Church of the Word," and the fact remains that the Protestant Christian goes to hear the preaching. Whether there are hundreds or very few present does not matter. The dissemination of what has happened is the essential element. But what if only the preacher and sexton should come to church, one might ask ironically. Well, if these two properly fulfill their roles, the one as preacher and the other as listener, there would be no room for irony, for they would represent the whole town at church. And of course such preaching is taken seriously in heaven. After all, the Lord of the church made the astonishing promise: "Where two or three are gathered in my name, there am I in the midst of them." (Matthew 18:20.)

Is Preaching the Word of God?

Our approach to preaching derives its significance and value from our belief in a God who has time for us and grants us His Word, a concept which is by no means self-evident. The great failing of us human fathers is that we have no time for our children. However, our Father in heaven has time; He takes time for us. We human fathers often neglect talking with our children. Although any ordinary farmhand knows how important it is to talk to cattle, some fathers do not know that they must talk with their children. We believe in a speaking God, as contrasted to false deities who are dumb. God descends and condescends to talk with us as a man speaks with men. He created all the creatures of the earth by means of His Word, but man He created *for* His Word, expressly to engage us in conversation in order to tell us what has taken place. He does this in two ways, so to speak, directly and indirectly. He speaks directly to the prophets and apostles; He also speaks through the servants of the Word who make use of the testimony of the apostles and prophets. Thus we have two beliefs: first, that the Word which God spoke to His

first-chosen servants really is His Word; and second, that
God also speaks through the expository words of preachers
in all ages, and that this, too, is His Word. Jesus said to His
disciples: "For it is not you who speak, but the Spirit of
your Father speaking through you" (Matthew 10:20), and
"He who hears you hears me" (Luke 10:16); therefore
people anywhere in all ages who sit at the feet of a preacher
may rightly believe with all their hearts that God is speaking
through the sermon. Thus the second Helvetian Confession
boldly states: "Praedicatio verbi Dei est verbum Dei"—"The
preaching of the Word *is* the Word of God." Everything is
dependent on the certainty of the preacher and the congregation that God speaks through the sermon. But, as I
have indicated, this belief is anything but self-evident. However, it is not a matter of false security but of certainty—of
what Paul often calls joyfulness. It was once said of Jesus
that He spoke "not as the scribes," but "as one who had
authority." (Mark 1:22.) If a preacher speaks like a scribe,
his preaching is clearly not God's Word. And now we are
faced with the mystery of authority. What is the basis of
authoritative preaching? How does preaching actually become the Word of God, and how does it happen that the
congregation can hear it as God's Word?

True authority (and there is such a thing as arrogated
authority!) is an act of grace. And the grace of God is free.
God can impart His Word, and He can withdraw it ma-
jestically. He can open the "door for the word" (Colossians
4:3), and He can also close it. When He opened the heart
of Lydia of Philippi, "to give heed to what was said by Paul"
(Acts 16:14), both the speaking of the apostle and the
listening of Lydia were a gift of grace. In the Old Testament it is often said, "And the word of the LORD came."

(Jeremiah 1:11.) Here His Word is referred to in terms of motion. "For he spoke, and it came to be; he commanded, and it stood forth." (Psalm 33:9.) Or, "So shall my word be that goes forth from my mouth; it shall not return to me empty, but it shall accomplish that which I purpose, and prosper in the thing for which I sent it." (Isaiah 55:11.) No man has the power to summon the presence of the Word of God. Here the preacher is distinguished from the sorcerer who thinks that he can compel God by chanting formulas. Both the preacher and the listener are dependent on grace. "I will be gracious to whom I will be gracious, and will show mercy on whom I will show mercy." (Exodus 33:19.) These words are equally true today.

Because God is free in the bestowal as well as the withdrawal of the Word, the "word of God can also be rare in the land." Or, stated another way, when farmers sowed seed by hand, they had to be sure that the wind was not blowing; a calm, still day was most desirable. The very opposite is required for the sowing of God's Word. Everything is dependent on the blowing of the wind. The Holy Spirit causes God's Word to come and not return empty but accomplish that which He purposes. But we must remember that the Holy Spirit is free, just as grace is free. Like the wind, the Holy Spirit can be present or absent. Christ said: "The wind blows where it wills, and you hear the sound of it, but you do not know whence it comes or whither it goes." (John 3:8.) This absolute freedom of grace and of the Holy Spirit makes us conscious of the overwhelming importance of prayer in connection with preaching and hearing.

Supplication for the Word

It sometimes happens that beginning ministers of the Word ask "how it is done." Their desire to learn how a sermon comes into being is entirely understandable; however, I must confess that such questions have caused me some embarrassment from time to time. Is this a question to which there is an answer? Is there a recipe for good preaching just as there are recipes for making pies or using the correct psychological techniques on difficult customers? Books have been written on public speaking which are instructive and of real value for those desiring to become successful pulpit orators. But is oratory really preaching? Can it be called the preaching of the Word of God? How does preaching come about? A Berlin student once asked me point-blank: "Please tell me the secret of your preaching." Finally I was only able to answer rather helplessly: "Poverty." The secret of all preaching is poverty, in the sense of the first beatitude. By this I mean that the act of preaching—and listening as well—is one of those things for which no one actually has true ability. The very moment a man thinks he has this ability, his preaching becomes art, and grace draws back in grief. To a certain extent, of course, the preacher must be an able man before he can prepare a proper sermon—here, however, is not the suitable place to discuss "mechanical tools"—but when a man really does have some ability, he becomes aware of the fact that he actually is not able, in the full sense of the word. After all sermon preparations are made, there still remains the decisive element, the gift of grace. Preaching is a gift, a supplication which has been granted. No less a man than Paul tells us that "our prophecy [that is, our preaching!] is imperfect." (1 Corinthians 13:9.) Paul planted, Apollos watered, but it was God who gave the growth.

We can now see the decisive contribution which the congregation of listeners makes in bringing about real preaching. Talk of the so-called passivity of the congregation is thoroughly imperceptive, and any member of the congregation with a knowledge of what preaching is knows that he is jointly responsible for every preaching service. Any preacher who does not have the support of a supplicating congregation will at best "speak like the scribes," or, what is even worse, he will speak like a pulpit orator. It is again Paul who, with noteworthy urgency, admonishes his churches to be faithful in their supplications for the service of the Word: "Pray at all times in the Spirit, with all prayer and supplication. To that end keep alert with all perseverance, making supplication for all the saints, and also for me, that utterance may be given me in opening my mouth boldly to proclaim the mystery of the gospel, for which I am an ambassador in chains; that I may declare it boldly, as I ought to speak." (Ephesians 6:18-20.) The apostle knows that all men, without exception, resist the preaching of the Word of God. In his reaction to the Word of God, man is like a house with a closed door. This door must open before the Word can enter, and it is not within the ability of the preacher to open this door. Neither psychology nor techniques of eloquence, neither suggestion nor logical proof, will open the door for the Word of God.

When Paul and Barnabas returned to Antioch from their first missionary journey and reported to the assembled believers whose supplicatory prayers had accompanied them, they made a most significant statement, a statement which

shows how preaching becomes effective: "They . . . declared
all that God had done with them, and how he had opened
a door of faith to the Gentiles." (Acts 14:27.) God alone can
act through the Holy Spirit in such a way that "faith comes
from what is heard, and what is heard comes by the preaching of Christ." (Romans 10:17.) God alone is able to open
the closed door. Immediately before the strong assertion
could be made later in Ephesus, "So the word of the Lord
grew and prevailed mightily," the reception of the Holy
Spirit was a matter of such urgent concern to the apostle
that he asked the few Christians whom he first met there,
"Did you receive the Holy Spirit . . .?" (Acts 19:20, 2.) Thus,
here as well, supplication for the Holy Spirit is prerequisite
for the growth and increase of the Word. Because the
apostle was convinced that not a single person comes to believe through the Word without the Holy Spirit, without
God's personal intervention, he told the believers elsewhere:
"Continue steadfastly in prayer, being watchful in it with
thanksgiving; and pray for us also, that God may open to us
a door for the word, to declare the mystery of Christ, on
account of which I am in prison, that I may make it clear,
as I ought to speak." (Colossians 4:2-4.) In view of such an
urgent request for supplicatory prayer, it is simply incon-
ceivable how anyone can still speak of purely passive participation by the congregation in the church service; a more
intensive spiritual activity is scarcely imaginable.

The Secret of Growth and of the Fruit

In his essay "Respect for the Word," Reinhold Schneider
points to the interesting distinction which Augustine draws

between voice and Word: "The word can do much, even without the voice; the voice is empty without the word." That is to say, our human voice is the tool of which God's Word makes use. If the Word of God is not present, there remains nothing but the human voice, which is empty and only a "mouth speaking great things." (Daniel 7:8.) These mouths speaking great things can be found in the pulpit, but they are nothing more than empty and hollow voices— voices without the Word. When the Word is absent the clergyman often tries to compensate by speaking loudly or by some other sort of substitute, whether it be cheap bids for popularity or belletristic utterances. For this reason, Augustine, in a variation on the well-known words of John the Baptist, makes the significant demand, "Let the voice decrease, and the word grow." If this admonition is not heeded and if only the voice fills the church instead of the Word—be it the best-trained bass or tenor—the fruit of the Word begins to stay away. Whoever does not check this danger with prayer and watchfulness will not preach well. A sense of security on the part of preachers is one reason that preaching so often becomes mere declamation or an empty voice, however orthodox the interpretation or high-church the celebration. At that point the word has ceased to be the Word, and judgment has begun in the house of God.

Whenever a group gathers for preaching and both they and the preacher have poverty of spirit, they may have the comforting joy that growth and fruit will be the result. This extremely happy expectation can point to a powerful, short parable of the Lord: "The kingdom of God is as if a man should scatter seed upon the ground, and should sleep and rise night and day, and the seed should sprout and grow, he knows not how. The earth produces of itself, first the blade, then the ear, then the full grain in the ear. But when the grain is ripe, at once he puts in the sickle, because the harvest has come." (Mark 4:26-29.) These are the joyous and full terms—one is tempted to add "succulent"—which Christ used in speaking of the much-reviled church of the "Word." In this parable the preached Word is promised a rich autumn with its overflowing fullness.

Above all, the fact that the seed does grow is of such overwhelming significance that it is absolutely impossible to imagine anything of even remotely the same importance which the preacher should add to this simple, great fact. In the face of this majestic promise we once again become aware of the secondary importance of what is usually called "methods of preaching." How do we preach to farmers and workers, to scholars and soldiers? How do we preach to young people, sick people, to Christians and heathen? In thoughtful tranquillity we should pay due respect to all these questions about the "how" of preaching, but of what value are all these questions and problems of method when measured against the all-eclipsing promise that we are dealing with seed which grows!

"It sprouts and grows, he knows not how." (Cf. Mark 4:27.) Even some preachers of the Word are among those who foolishly complain that, unlike the carpenter or shoemaker, they cannot tally their accomplishments at the end of a day's work—as if even the artisan could make such a reckoning at the snap of a finger! But the preacher should be the last to try to take inventory of the results of his work. Biblically speaking, a census is a thing of the heathen, and so we must be cautious in our church census. Counting the congregation is among the secret sins of preachers and, as a matter of fact, of many a church member as well. Christ said of the seed, it grows, "he knows not how," and obviously the preacher is not supposed to know how. For of course if a minister of the Word could be absolutely certain that his preaching was solely responsible for the salvation of even one single person there would be grounds enough for pride, and the devil would have his finger in it. That the sower is not supposed to know the seed is growing is naturally a source of sorrow for him, but it is significant and salutory—in fact, it is a blessing. And of course faith may have the certainty that the Kingdom of God is growing where and when it is not observed. Indeed, according to Scripture, it often grows in just those times and at just those places where we humans can see only withering, retrogression, and collapse—the very opposites of growth in the eyes of man. Divine growth and human success are two entirely different things.

We are no less surprised, in fact we are actually astonished, to read that the seed can grow even when the sower lies down to sleep after his day's work. Only God will "neither slumber nor sleep." (Psalm 121:4.) God can send us off to bed like little children and His Kingdom will still grow; it is this fact which ends all ministerial self-importance. There was once a man who thought he should not sleep lest the work of God come to a stop. But God called out to this supposedly indispensable man: "Extinguish the lamp, the Kingdom of God will by no means perish because of it." Yes, when the night is stillest, there can develop the most vigorous growth in the Kingdom of God. "He gives to his beloved in sleep." (Psalm 127:2.) And if the night should come "when no one can work" (John 9:4), then, according to the promise, the Kingdom more than ever will develop into perfection.

We are reminded of that strange Generalissimo, Kutuzov,

portrayed by Tolstoy in *War and Peace*. The Czar had given
Kutuzov the terrible task of engaging Napoleon's forces before Moscow. On the evening before the battle, Tolstoy
depicts the General bent over plans and unrolled maps, at
headquarters with his staff. But toward midnight there came
from the general's chair the sound of snoring, soft at first
but louder with each passing moment. Surrounded by officers engaged in vigorous debate, at one o'clock Kutuzov
awakened, pulled out his watch ceremoniously, stood up and
said: "Gentlemen, we shall all do our duty, but I think we
need to have slept before the battle." Kutuzov lost that
battle. But the victor of the battle, who always made do
with little sleep, finally lost the war. Kutuzov had the
greater endurance. In view of the havoc which our Protestant activity causes, it might not be superfluous to consider that "we need to have slept before the battle." By this
I mean quite simply that what we need are silent pastors,
not hustlers. A few days ago I read something in an annual
report which was like a sign of judgment on the Protestant
house of God. A clergyman who left his parish twenty
years ago and who since has worked in another job with
great blessing, now says that he had to leave his pastorate
at that time in order to have the opportunity to read and
interpret the Bible. Things had reached such a point that he
had to flee from his parish to be a minister of the Word! We
sorely need pastors who read the Bible, pray, and preach
God's Word; we need pastors whose congregations give
them time to perform that service on which all else depends
—ministry of the Word.

Finally, the Lord of the harvest sends out the sickle. In
the language of the Apocalypse, the sickle is the sign of
judgment and can easily be seen glistening throughout

Christendom. But when in secret faithfulness that seed is sowed which grows and bears fruit secretly through the Holy Spirit, the time of the sickle is the sign of the gracious judgment of God. The time of the sickle will inevitably bring to light what was only sound, but it will also reveal what was the Word that bore fruit—thirty, sixty, a hundred-fold.

What Shall I Preach?

"A voice says, 'Cry!' And I said, 'What shall I cry?'" (Isaiah 40:5.)* From the first witnesses to present-day ministers of the Word, men have wondered about the subject matter for their preaching, a central question which we shall now consider. What is it all about when a congregation goes to hear preaching on Sunday or a weekday? What is the justification for the whole expenditure, the ringing of the bells, the urgency with which this invitation is directed to all the people? Why do we wear our best clothes to church? Suppose a stranger from another part of the world entered an evangelical church for the first time and asked what purpose the building served and what was going on inside. What would be our answer? What does go on when there is preaching?

In our efforts to arrive at the most accurate answer possible, we shall not begrudge a short linguistic digression. In an article in Kittel's New Testament dictionary, Gerhard Friedrich points to the messenger of victory who occurs in the military history of almost every nation. This figure is also to be found among the ancient Greeks who are known

* In the German translation of this passage, the word is *predige* (preach).

for their ability to relate their history and celebrate their heroes in song. The best-known messenger of victory was the one who, after the battle of Marathon, reportedly brought the news to Athens of the victory over the Persians with such speed that he fell dead on arriving. In memory of this messenger of victory we have the "Marathon" in the sports world of today, a race of 42.2 kilometers. Such a messenger reported to the anxious citizens of the city the outcome of the battle and, if possible, the number of enemies killed and captured. Upon reaching his destination, he raised his hand in greeting and called out with a loud voice; *"Chaire, nikomen"*—"Greetings, the victory is ours!" He could come by ship, by horse, or on foot. Even from afar his appearance betrayed his good news. His face beamed, the point of his lance was decorated with foliage, and he wore a wreath on his head. The messenger always tried to be the first to arrive with the news; every possible effort was made to reduce the agonizing period of uncertainty suffered by the waiting city. Deliberate delay was punished, but speed was duly rewarded. Of course we are familiar with this messenger of joy not only in conjunction with war and victory but also in private life. We need think only of the nurse who announces the birth of a child or of the messenger who tells a candidate that he has been elected to office. In any event, these messengers of victory and good news are bright figures, and what they have to report is joy. The ancient Greeks had a special expression for them; they were called *Euángelos* or *Euangelístes*. The act of transmitting the news was called *Euangelízesthai*, and the report of victory, the good news which they bore, was called *Euangélion*.

The Christians of the early period were faced with the task of making known the good news of Christ to a world

in which Greek was largely spoken. When they had to trans-
late the good news into Greek, they made use of these ex-
pressive words already in existence. How stirring it is that
these very words seem to have expressed most accurately
what the Christians wanted to communicate to their listeners about the news of Christ. In the preacher of the Word
they saw a messenger of victory and of good news. Thus the
word "evangel" and related words denote "report of victory."* The word *Euangélion* occurs four times in Luke,
eight times in Matthew, and over sixty times in the writings
of the apostle Paul. From the choice of these words we can
clearly see what preaching is. The bells are rung because
all the people are to hear the report of victory. To be sure, it
is not the victory of Marathon or of any other historic battle-
field which is being reported; it is the victory of Jerusalem—
or to be more exact, it is the victory of Golgotha, the victory
of Good Friday with the words "It is finished," and the
victory of Easter with the words "He has risen." On Good
Friday Christ conquered hell; on Easter day He overcame
death; He lives, rules, and will come again. All these events
have happened; they have taken place. We are not dealing
with a victory of man over men. This is nothing less than
the victory of God over men and forces—the victory of
heaven over hell for the sake of the world. This victory is
what preaching may and must report. Nearly a century ago
Blumhardt freshly and powerfully emphasized precisely this
point as the subject matter of all Christian preaching when
he issued the announcement, "Jesus is victor."

* This illustration is even more striking in the German, where *Evangelium*
is the usual word for "gospel."

Preaching as Offense

One might now conclude that there can be nothing more sublime in all the world than to be such a messenger of victory and joy, and he may well find this true. "If anyone aspires to the office of bishop [the office of preacher is meant here, since the deacon is mentioned immediately following], he desires a noble task." (1 Timothy 3:1.) And yet we notice even in the Old Testament how often words of encouragement are called out to the messengers of good news. One messenger was told that he was not to be afraid, and another was told that he was not to allow his mouth to be stopped but was to speak. As often as Jesus spoke to His messengers of their future ministry of the Word, He placed before them the prospect of suffering and, at the same time, of help in their distress. Paul, too, knew much about fear and shame in the ministry of the Word.

What, we may very well wonder, could there be in this ministry as a messenger of victory which causes shame and arouses fear? In considering this question we must remember that there are special circumstances surrounding the Victor of Jerusalem. The victory of Golgotha is hidden, enveloped in mystery, and veiled past recognition. The naked eye sees a man who has been bound, terribly tortured, cruelly mocked and crucified—a man who began big and ended small. One sees a defeated man, a dead Jew, the very opposite of what is usually meant by the words "triumphant victor." That this Jesus on the cross is a victor can be grasped only with faith. From this truth comes the great offense of Christian preaching, an offense which must be affirmed and overcome in faith. And so Paul writes to the Corinthians:

"When I came to you, brethren, I did not come proclaiming to you the testimony of God in lofty words or wisdom. For I decided to know nothing among you except Jesus Christ and him crucified." (1 Corinthians 2:1-2.) Despite the offense involved, Paul does not intend to be ashamed of the message that Jesus the crucified is Jesus the Victor. Thus, preaching means believing and taking the stand that He on the cross is the Victor nevertheless. The messenger of victory has no available proof for the truth of his report. Quite to the contrary, men find enough so-called proof which seems to refute such a message. Like Paul, the preacher can only deliver his message quite simply and without defense, and when asked for proof he can once again declare, despite all offense, that he believes in the victory of Him crucified and, moreover, that he has confidence that He who has risen will Himself furnish the proof that He lives. For the man who believes that Christ has risen, preaching is a noble task.

Neither Christ Himself nor His messengers appear to be victors. The man who bears the tidings of victory is himself not the victor. Instead, he is among the conquered and vanquished, even though he believes in Christ the Victor. The face of this messenger of victory does not beam; the point of his lance is perhaps wretchedly broken off, not decorated; and he will hardly wear a wreath on his head as did the messengers of ancient Greece. How much occasion there was to be offended at the infirmity of the messenger Paul! Evidence of this offense can be found especially in the second letter to the Corinthians. The people who took offense at the lowliness of this messenger of victory went so far as to say of him: "His letters are weighty and strong, but his bodily presence is weak, and his speech of no account." (2 Corinthians 10:10.) He bore the thorn in his flesh, was struck by the fists of Satan, and for long years was a man who wore chains. But "When I am weak, then I am strong." (2 Corinthians 12:10.) And "Thanks be to God, who in Christ always leads us in triumph, and through us spreads the fragrance of the knowledge of him everywhere." (2 Corinthians 2:14.)

Not only the Victor and the messenger of victory, but also the recipients of the message give plentiful occasion for offense; the congregation itself looks more like a band of defeated people than a victorious army. They are a small herd and a herd of the small. They have "this treasure in earthen vessels" (2 Corinthians 4:7), in fragile dishes. The apostle says of his hearers as well as of himself that they are "always carrying in the body the death of Jesus." (2 Corinthians 4:10.) But then he continues, admonishing the suffering church to victory, "so that the life of Jesus may also be manifested in our bodies." Thus in Christian preaching a band of miserable and burdened people testify that Jesus is Victor. Consequently, only with faith which neither feels nor sees can we be preachers and hearers of the Word. If it were not for faith, preaching would be the most paradoxical occupation in God's world. Visualize the situation for just one moment: the seemingly vanquished brings news of victory!

Attacks on Preaching

We have just considered the most essential and far-reaching reason for the offense of preaching. However, preaching is attacked for many other reasons and in all possible forms, and these attacks must be withstood and endured. Ministry of the Word is most frequently assailed

in the name of action, of deed. In his *Faust,* Goethe permitted himself an abrupt correction of the beginning of the
Gospel according to John, "In the beginning was the word";
he wrote, "In the beginning was the deed." Faust has found
many successors in the nineteenth and twentieth centuries.
Soon after the Second World War, the western world was
faced with the tragic fact that the world was hungry. In his
inaugural speech before an international charity organization of which he had been elected president, the first words
of Mayor La Guardia of New York were: "Give me plows,
not typewriters." Waving a fat sheaf of well-stated written
promises from forty-four different countries which had
pledged assistance, La Guardia continued: "Bread is better
than resolutions." In this instance he was right, only too
right! There are situations in which plows actually are better
than typewriters and bread better than resolutions, for good
deeds are always preferable to bad words. But when such
statements are made by those for whom materialism is a
basic principle—and we are sufficiently familiar with such
beliefs—they constitute an attack on the Word of God and
thus on the ministry of the Word. It is then that the plow
vaunts itself in the face of the typewriter, the instrument of
words. Soon, angrily and with disdain, daily bread stands in
full battle array against Sunday resolutions. In this connection we think of a well-known character on the contemporary scene; his name is "tractor," and he is one of the idols
of this century. At the same time we hear the expression,
"just preaching."

Not only under attack by unbelievers outside the church,
preaching is also assailed by those of little faith within the
church. It was a minister of the Word—as a matter of fact, a
man who for a long time was entrusted with training preach-

ers at one of our theological institutions—who expressed
grave doubts as to whether the man of today can be reached
at all by preaching. When we remember what the Holy
Scripture tells us about the content of Christian preaching,
must we not be greatly concerned about a church which, in
the opinion of one of its theologians, must consider the fact
that the "man of today simply cannot be reached by a
church which only preaches"? We cannot but ask: how on
earth is this "man of today" to be reached, if not through
tidings of victory and joy? Is the "man of today" a race apart
from those men who have the continuing promise that faith
comes from preaching? Our misgivings do not lessen when
the same theologian states: "Evangelical charity work is
probably the most gratifying thing to be seen in the church
of our time." Such words, contrasted to the "church which
only preaches," basically assert that the man of today cannot be reached by preaching, but that he can perhaps be
approached through service. Without doubt, these words
were said with an eye to the public, for such talk can count
on agreement among Christians, Jews, Moslems, and
heathen. Again we have the plow instead of the typewriter
—this time from the mouth of a churchman. Whoever cannot rid himself of the illusion that the church can reach the
man of today through signs and miracles rather than through
the poverty of the disdained Word, and whoever believes
that the church can be more effective through charity than
preaching should, for a moment, remember the extent of
faith at those places where Christ Himself performed so
many deeds and signs. Think of the cities by the sea, particularly Capernaum!

In light of the Holy Scripture we can see absolutely no
other way for man, including the "man of today," to be

brought to faith except through the abiding stewardship of the mysteries of God and through the communication of the news of victory—and this means preaching. It is, of course, true that men have always closed their ears to the Word; this is no phenomenon peculiar to our times alone. But the reason man closes his ears is not because he simply cannot be reached by the Word, but rather because he is immersed in the dark mystery of impenitence and because we have not preached with authority the Word that bears fruit. Service? Yes, in its place and as an act of thankfulness and as the fruit of authoritative preaching. But service as the way to the "man of today," or service even as a substitute for preaching? No! Of course, it is true that good—really good —deeds are preferable to really bad preaching, but note that the situation is sometimes reversed so that deeds can be bad, really bad, while the words are good. The Old and New Testaments know of a good Word. It is good and will survive "all things of the flesh" because, as we saw, it is the Word of victory, the good news, the evangel. No more urgent and indispensable service is conceivable than this service of reporting, even in the age of the tractor. What would be left if the ministry of the Word should cease?

Preaching as Teaching

Preaching can and should be instructive, but this phase of preaching presents us with difficulties. Has not ordinary preaching been too didactic, at least in our own lifespan? Has it not been a symptom of our sickness that our preaching, anything but a message of victory, has been dwindling off to dull lectures? If Roman Catholic churches have the

odor of incense, have our evangelical churches not had the
aroma of the schoolhouse, or perhaps even of the syna-
gogue? And yet teaching is a part of preaching if done in the
right sense and the proper spirit. There is such a thing as
legalistic teaching, and the law kills. However, we have
often wished that what we were hearing actually was the
law and not morality, as has so often been the case. In many
instances our preaching has become moralistic. However,
teaching does not necessarily have to be moralistic in content. Instructive preaching may and should concern itself
with the message of victory and glad tidings, and with nothing else. Even when teaching becomes admonition, it is
admonition in Christ. Paul's words to the Colossians will
serve to instruct us: "Teach and admonish one another in all
wisdom, and . . . sing psalms and hymns and spiritual songs
. . . in your hearts to God." (Colossians 3:16.) How surprising and cheering, how essential, that teaching and even
admonition are placed in such proximity to the singing and
playing of "psalms and hymns and spiritual songs." Teaching is blessed when it deals with the joy of thankfulness and
the splendor of the praise of God, not when it treats dead
ideas and obscure and ambiguous truths. Even admonition
does not need to be based on the rigid morality of the
schoolmaster or parson; it should spring from thanks and
exultation over God's victory on Good Friday and Easter.
And so instruction and admonition will also comfort and
edify. The grace which is new every morning "has no end
the whole day," or the whole week through. When the evangelical Christian hears a sermon, he should be taught, ad-
monished, strengthened, edified, comforted, and lifted up.

The teaching sermon certainly does not consist of lecturing the congregation on dogmatics, important as it is that

our higher institutions of learning offer such instruction and that our preachers take due cognizance of it. It is not good to use love as an excuse for scorning knowledge and instructive pursuit of truth, but work in dogmatics belongs in the study. Dogmatics should be imbedded in the sermon like iron rods in reinforced concrete. Even though there is no place in the pulpit for doctrinal lecturing, there is another form of teaching entirely suitable for the congregation—narration. Particularly in these days of minimal Biblical knowledge, the importance of instructive narration can hardly be overestimated. One might ask what is to be narrated. During the period of the group movement it was once said that the laity of the church, the church member, could not preach—that was not his affair—but he could do something else; he could narrate. Of course that idea drew a certain distinction between preaching and narrating, but as a means of instruction, narration very definitely has its place in evangelical preaching. The subject of the narration is, of course, the crucial question. Should one talk about himself, or should he not again and again tell of the victory of God? We read that after Pentecost the Christians "devoted themselves to the apostles' teaching." (Acts 2:42.) What was the substance of this teaching? These were men who had just been saved, and when a stranger has saved our life, we naturally experience the strong desire to become acquainted with this savior. The apostles satisfied this desire on the part of the people. They told of the work and person of this Saviour; they told of what they themselves had seen and heard, of what they had seen with their eyes and had touched with their own hands. They told of the words and deeds of God in the Old Testament, which all pointed to the deeds and words of Christ. They told how He went to the cross, how He rose again, and how He went to the Father whence He shall come again. And those who had been saved listened gladly as they were told of their Saviour and His works. This narrating which instructs and illuminates is a part of preaching. The long sermon text has assumed real importance in our day; simply because it is read before the congregation it imparts more knowledge of the Bible than the few short verses of the "springboard" text which place the real words of the Bible in the background and for the most part spotlight the ingeniousness of the preacher. It is a special gift if now and again a congregation can hear the reading of an entire book of the Bible in one sitting. The best thing to be heard from the pulpit—and this occurs principally on feast days—is still the simple retelling of the event which is being commemorated. The Victor of Jerusalem Himself, of whom it is said that He is the same yesterday, today, and in all eternity, will see to it that these narrations are of living events, not of dead history.

The Prophetic Word

It is true that a preacher is not a prophet. And the warning, "Let not many of you become teachers" (James 3:1), is even more applicable to the claim of prophecy: "Let not many of you become prophets." It is also true that not only the office of the twelve apostles but also the use of God-commissioned prophets as instruments is limited to the Bible, but we do notice mention of "teachers and prophets" aside from the original twelve. The teachers were probably former priests who, with their gift of the knowledge of the Old Testament, served the congregations as scribes. The prophets, however, were believers filled with the Holy Spirit. Led and driven by the Holy Spirit, they were commissioned by God and in His name were able to say what should be done or left undone in a particular, concrete situation. In other words, teachers give general instruction while prophets give concrete directions. However, awareness of the fact that we are not prophets must not lead to false modesty or provide us with an excuse, consciously or unconsciously, for evading an uncomfortable task. Each sermon preached today can have prophetic significance, so to speak, and can also have prophetic effects. This is the case only because there are prophetic books in the Bible which long to be treated as more than historical incidents not binding on us; these books are waiting to be interpreted to our time, waiting to be preached. We note that these prophetic books have their times of particular significance. It can happen that one particular book, quite on its own, begins to speak to a particular period, indeed, to cry out. In tense times the sparks of the Spirit flash from the words of the old prophets just as electricity begins to crackle from the hair of an Alpine climber during a severe electric storm.

Late in the summer of 1940 the editorial staff of the *Basler Kirchenboten* periodical was reprimanded by the censors for printing verbatim a chapter from the book of Habakkuk. There are times and places where the words of the prophets speak with special clarity, and the preacher's task consists largely in not weakening or twisting the words of the prophets which speak for themselves. If texts are selected on the basis of one's own subjective will or are set by church authorities, the prophetic ministry of the Word will be affected disastrously. How many highly explosive Biblical words never reach the ears of the congregation simply because of this selective use of the Bible! Church officials and individual ministers of the Word are accustomed to circumventing and leaving alone "dangerous" Bible words as cautiously as though they were enemy strongholds. Or, expressed differently, how can arrogated prophesying feel sufficiently attracted to such "dangerous" Bible words in order to light upon them, whether the occasion be suitable or not! Self-determined selecting from the Bible makes too much room for human intention and managing. It has been said that the preacher is commissioned to sow, not to shoot, and this is very true. When one's own choice of text is avoided as much as possible through exposition of whole chapters and books, preaching will lose the character of shooting and become sowing, even when explosive texts are being treated. And every now and then the preacher and the congregation have the happy feeling that it is not we who choose the text, but the text which chooses us—so active, living, and powerful is the Word. Thus we see that under no circumstances is the prophetic ministry of the Word a matter of the preacher himself creating out of the Word; rather he must let the Word take its prophetic effect in the realm of testifying and professing, as it can do, and must neither pass over it in silence nor render it innocuous. As a result, when special conditions demand it, the Word itself professes, and to conceal the Word when the occasion arises to profess it amounts to denying the Word. There is much such silent denial regarding conditions and events in the church and in the world. But when the preacher and the congregation do not withdraw from the prophetic ministry of professing when God's hour demands it, this ministry can become witnessing. However, it can have as its consequence suffering, struggle, and loneliness. Such suffering which results from professing is grace, not the work of man, and much human weakness and refusal are involved. In reality, Luther's well-known statement, "Here I stand, I can do no other," in most cases should rather be, "Here I kneel, I can do no other." In such suffering, Christ proves to be powerful and helpful. "For as we share abundantly in Christ's sufferings, so through Christ we share abundantly in comfort too." (2 Corinthians 1:5.) And, finally, the congregations under the cross, preachers and listeners, will do well to expect no help from men—very often they need not expect even the support of church authorities.

In our consideration of the prophetic ministry of the Word we must note that silence is not always merely a form of denial; it can be prophetic as well. In times of turmoil, when the waves of national upheaval beat high, it is not good to allow one's self to be picked up by the ground waves and carried along like a surfboard rider. The "word for the occasion" can consist of deliberately saying nothing which would elicit surprise and indignation. In times of general hysteria, keeping silent can be the need of the hour. At several crucial times Karl Barth has exercised such prophetic silence. The preacher may follow the daily press attentively, but one reason is in order that his preaching not sound like the newspapers. Although out of context, the word from the passion of Christ can serve as a model for us: "But Jesus was silent."

Preaching as Worship

Sometimes at sports events a moment of silence is observed in honor of the victor. Something of this tradition also has its place in Christian preaching. He whom we honor is Christ, the last Victor over the last enemy. The worshipful veneration of the Victor is carried out by prayer and song, likewise part of the preached Word. In this discussion there is not space enough to consider prayer and song in church services, but again and again the preached Word becomes worship quite aside from prayer and song. Many passages of praise and adoration come to our attention when we read the books of the Bible. In the midst of the terrible upbraiding which the Lord had to pronounce upon the unrepentent cities by the sea, He suddenly and mysteriously burst forth with words of worship: "I thank thee, Father, Lord of heaven and earth, that thou hast hidden these things from the wise and understanding and revealed them to babes; yea, Father, for such was thy gracious will." (Matthew 11:25-26.) The chapters on the mystery of Israel (Romans 9-11) culminate in words of adoration: "O the depth of the riches and wisdom and knowledge of God" (Romans 11:33); and the chapter on the resurrection reaches its zenith in the cry of exultation and praise: "But thanks be to God, who gives us the victory through our Lord Jesus Christ" (1 Corinthians 15:57). This outburst of worship will take place in all preaching which is blessed, authoritative, and effected by the Spirit. But in reality it is not an outburst from down below to up above; rather it is a breaking through from that "higher choir," from that land where "no longer shall each man teach . . . his brother" (Jeremiah 31:34), where continual praise and eternal adoration rule. The whole last book of the Holy Scripture, which deals with the church under attack, is one single expression of adoration and shows us this mysterious superimposition and entwining of the worship of God which takes place in heaven as well as on earth.

In this book of the Bible the twenty-four elders bring before the throne of God "golden bowls full of incense, which are the prayers of the saints; and they sang a new song" (Revelation 5:8-9.) These twenty-four elders represent the earthly church in heaven and present before God our worship of Him. Both worship services, the one here and the one in heaven, are one and the same. The small band, the miserable group which gathers down here for preaching, has its part in the service in heaven. The church which fights here corresponds to the triumphant church in heaven. The message of victory, offensive and under attack, the good tidings which have been dampened by struggle and sorrow on earth, are expressed in heaven with rejoicing and splendor. The miserable and burdened who on earth hear the preaching of the Word and who are present when worship is expressed in prayer, words, and song are indeed aware of their imprisonment, but they know that they are "prisoners of Zion"; that is, that their "mouths will be full of laughter and their tongues full of praise." (Cf. Psalm 126:2.)

During the last war a certain small town suffered an air raid. On the following Sunday, a miserable group of survivors gathered together at church time on the village square where formerly the church had stood. They pulled charred hymnals from the still smoking ruins, someone read a Psalm, and then they prayed and sang a hymn. Heroism? No, this was worship breaking through from above! No bells had rung, the organ pipes had melted, no clergyman was present, but there stood the congregation worshiping through the Word.

EVANGELICAL
CONFESSION

Eduard Thurneysen

Evangelical Confession

ONE OF THE SIGNS of our times is that the *desire for confession* is even breaking out in the evangelical church of today. The theme "confession" was treated by a special study group at the evangelical church assembly held in Frankfurt in 1956. Every opportunity for confession was offered at this assembly, and a great many people availed themselves of it.

"Leben und Glauben" ("Life and Faith"), an evangelical weekly with wide circulation in Switzerland, commented as follows: "The leadership of the German church assembly has dared to take this radical step in public. Not only was 'confession' made a discussion topic, but also approximately thirty places were set up in Frankfurt where private confessions could be heard. One evening seventy people came to one such site, and two more places for confession had to be improvised. At another location the confessor had to remain at his post until midnight to accommodate all those desirous of confessing."

But even aside from this event, anyone associated with the ministry can confirm the fact that the desire for confession exists both within and without the church. We are said to lack the opportunity for it in the evangelical church, and our Catholic fellow Christians are envied the confessionals in all their churches. In fact, the Catholic Church wins some converts because it offers the opportunity for confession. Confession-movements are arising within the

evangelical church; we need mention only the group movement and point to the recently formed brotherhoods and
sisterhoods of Taizé, Grandchamp, and Darmstadt, which
practice confession regularly. Evangelical theological litera-
ture also contains new treatments of confession; for example,
Beichtlehre für evangelische Christen ("System of Confession for Evangelical Christians") by Wolfgang Böhme, *Der
verlorene Schlüssel* ("The Lost Key") by Thomas Kronholz,
and *Evangelisches Beichtbüchlein* ("Evangelical Booklet of
Confession") by Oskar Planck. And finally we must remember that confession of a sort plays a role in psychotherapy,
in secular form to be sure.

We notice that this is *private confession* which we are
encountering; it is not the counsel of a ministrant or the
psychological clarification of difficult problems of life, nor
is it the prayer of confession and assurance of pardon in
which the whole congregation participates at church services. People want to disclose their sins before a confessor
and hear from him the promise of absolution. What is behind this desire? It is caused by the deep disquietude with
life which has beset modern man; it is the failure to come to
terms with one's self, an inability to live which man cannot
overcome with his own strength. The prayer of confession
at church services and conversation with the minister are
not sufficient. If ministry is going to exist, it must take place
in the form of personal private confession which is either
supposedly or actually more intense and concentrated. And
it cannot be merely one's neighbor who hears the confession.
It must be the pastor, that is, a holder of church office, to
whom alone has been entrusted the special authority necessary to hear confessions and grant forgiveness. In order to

give expression to this authority, the office-holder will don his official attire for the confession, the robe, and when possible receive the confesser in the church. Perhaps he will even erect a crucifix and light candles; in any event he will make use of a definite liturgical formula for the confession. All of this can be read in instructions for confession recently drawn up by members of the evangelical church.

But what does all this mean? Are we not near, terribly near, the practice of confession of the Catholic Church? To be sure, in the Catholic Church confession is not merely offered, it is demanded, and it is the priest and only the priest who has the power to determine sins and give absolution by virtue of his ordination. But the fathers of our church have completely severed us from this institution and practice of confession, which is one of the ineffaceable lines of division between the evangelical and Catholic churches. When confessing becomes a law, the freedom of grace is encroached upon. When the priest and he alone can remit sins, the evangel is pushed aside. For according to the gospel it is *Christ* and Christ *alone* who forgives sins. He is the true "priest" to whom we may bring our sins, because He alone can remove them from us. Since He has suffered for us on the cross, it is only He, He Himself, before whom we can lay down our trespasses. In all seriousness we must ask whether those in our evangelical church who wish confession to the pastor to be introduced as an established institution will not involuntarily grant ingress to the error of Rome.

Let us now examine the concept of confession and consider how it should properly be practiced. In the final analysis, does it hold that real confession can be practiced in no form other than that used by the Catholic Church? If this is true, it would be better for the evangelical church never again to use the word "confession." In any event, we must use this word with the greatest of caution. If we should use "confession" in the Roman Catholic sense, the term "evangelical confession" would be self-contradictory, because the gospel and confession to a priest are mutually exclusive. The concept of "confession" is in the same situation as the concept of "sacrament," which in the Catholic Church is inseparably linked with confession. Unfortunately, the revivers of confession in our church have no hesitation in calling their "evangelical confession" a "sacrament." However, we shall not quibble about words. The question of confession must certainly be detached from Catholic misuse; if so, we may then use the word "confession," because it already exists as a word and because it is almost impossible to discuss confession without using the word "confession." And so the word will be used in this discussion, with, however, the reservations indicated above.

Let us now examine this matter of confession. What does it mean, what is it? We shall begin by considering the literal meaning of the German verb *beichten*. It is not a Biblical term and cannot be found in a Bible dictionary. The word comes from Old High German *bigiht* which means to affirm something, to stand for something, not only to one's self in private but to do it aloud and before witnesses. This public affirming can best be rendered by the word *bekennen* —to admit, acknowledge, to own up to something. This is a concept frequently used in both the Old and the New Testaments and consequently is the word which most precisely conveys what *beichten* means. Latin, English, and French use the words *confessio* and "confession" for *beichten*.* In confession we acknowledge *sin*. The idea of confession is that it is the admission of sin. "I confess" means: I own up to something definite that I have done and for which I am responsible. It has the meaning of being responsible for something, in contrast to a fate which one merely suffers. I admit, I affirm this my deed, but in such a fashion that it becomes clear that I have done it under the domination of sin. My deed bears the mark of sin just as manufactured products have trademarks which point to their origin. The peculiar thing about sin, whether it be subtle or gross, external or internal, open or secret, is that something like a strange power takes hold of me, carrying me where I do not want to go; but I say "yes" to it, I am the one who does it, I cannot shift the responsibility to the strange power, I myself am sinful. In the garb of my own deed the strange power of sin takes up lodging with me, as it were. And now I am its prisoner. I do something and something quite brutal happens to me and with me, in and with my doing—these two happenings are actually one and the same. This is the situation to which the apostle gives expression when he cries out: "For I do not do what I want, but I do the very thing I hate." (Romans 7:15.) But the fact remains that I do it! I do the sin. Standing up to it, bringing it to light, admitting it—that is the meaning of confessing.

But what is the purpose of confessing? How should it help

* Although not exact equivalents, "to confess" and "confession" will be used as translations of *beichten* and its noun form *Beichte* which normally refer only to the confession of one's sins, particularly in the confessional. The word *bekennen* and its derivatives will be translated by "to admit," "profess," "acknowledge," and "own up." The distinction which Thurneysen makes here is of course more striking in German where the word *beichten* has a more specialized meaning than the English "confess."

to admit to a sin? Can I free myself from sin by my admission? Do I break out of the imprisonment of my sin by proclaiming it to myself or to another man? Sin calls for forgiveness, but can I forgive myself, can another person forgive my sin? Only one, only *God,* can forgive. For this reason, confession as such is an empty act, unless it is directed to God. When we speak of sin we very certainly speak of God. There is such a thing as sin only because God exists. If there were no God, there would also be no sin. By virtue of its very nature, sin is something which takes place between God and me. To be sure, when we think of the word "sin" we think primarily of definite individual sins, such as prevarication, theft, or adultery. But we must learn to distinguish between sin and sins. Lying, stealing, and adultery are sins, but these sins are, so to speak, the fruits, the expressions, the consequences of the *one* sin which is the root and source of all these sins. This "root sin," the primary and first sin, is an event between God and ourselves: the turning away of our hearts from Him. Sin is the audacious attempt, undertaken time and time again, to live our lives without God. Doubt in God and in His commands and the insolent question whether man himself cannot determine what is good and bad—this is the description of sin in the account of the fall (Genesis 3), that basic passage in the Bible where sin is mentioned for the first time. With all our sins we are sinful before God. Thus confession is genuine and true only when it places us before God as before our judge. Consequently, there is no real confession which does not become prayer, indeed, which is not in itself a prayer. Thus the words of the Psalm: "Against thee, thee only, have I sinned, and done that which is evil in thy sight." (Psalm 51:4.) Praying, calling out, crying in this way—that is, crying before God, calling to Him—that and that alone is confession.

But how could we confess if we did not know that *God forgives!* We must first grasp this basic concept if we want to understand what confession is. Confessing means carrying one's sins before God, but it means carrying them before that God who is merciful beyond all comprehension. Let us now think of the word "evangelical" which we placed before the word "confession." The evangel means and is the message of grace, for it means and is the message of the forgiveness of sins. Indeed, it is the message of *Jesus Christ.* Can anything else, anything more inclusive, greater and truer, be said of Jesus than this one thing: He forgives! In Jesus, God gave especially tangible evidence of His love for man. God loves us men, He does not bargain with us. There is no trading, no business dealing, between God and man, according to which we would have to do something in order to receive forgiveness. Forgiveness would not be forgiveness if it were not a free gift of God. Thus our confessing is never to be understood as a human deed which we have to perform in order only then to have God act upon us. When the paralytic was brought before Jesus, there was no confession first; immediately the word of forgiveness was given to him: "Your sins are forgiven." (Matthew 9:2.) This was an act of free grace, without a preliminary acknowledgment of sins. What God in His grace does for us has need of no preliminary action, assistance, or supplementation on our part.

Here again we differ from the *Catholic* doctrine of confession which demands contrition and the enumeration of individual sins as a preliminary action to be followed by definite acts of penance imposed by the priest. *Evangelical* confessing, however, knows nothing but the great preliminary action of Christ and the advantage which He has given us. All that we do in our confessing—to which certainly belong the acknowledgment of our sin, our penitence, and our repentance—takes place only as an action subsequent to what Christ has already done for us and subsequent to what makes our confession possible in the first place.

Viewed outwardly and chronologically, the act of confessing may seem to come first, but in its essence, in its inner execution, it is completely subsequent to Christ's act. Confession comes from sheer thankfulness, it comes from realization of grace and it comes as praise and glory of that grace which has dawned above us in Christ—this is all that confession is. For this reason confessing must remain a joyful act, it must be done completely voluntarily, must by no means be imposed by any law, and must never take place in compliance with a method through which we should like to procure grace for ourselves. To be sure, the whole seriousness of the judgment of God stands before us, but at the same time and all of a sudden He stands before us, Christ, who sets aright our judgment inasmuch as He has borne it for us. What does the catechism say of the judgment of God? It *comforts* me—so the catechism dares to say—because, "with uplifted head I look for the very same person who offered himself, for my sake, to the tribunal of God, and hath removed all curse from me, to come as judge from heaven." (*Heidelberg Catechism*, Question 52.)* Thus if something is to be omitted from the practice of confession it is the portrayal without grace of the terrors of hell cus-

* This translation is quoted from: *The Heidelberg Catechism, Or a Summary of Christian Doctrine as Used by the German Reformed Church in the United States of America* (Baltimore, 1849).

tomarily pictured even today by not only the Catholic but
also the evangelical preacher of confession and repentance.
Consideration is not taken of the fact that although the
gospel speaks of judgment and condemnation, these words
are from the mouth of Him who has come to bolt the doors
of hell and take condemnation from us. Of course, whoever
looks away from Him, from Christ, for even a moment has
every reason to be terrified of condemnation and hell. But
who tells us to look away from Him? To look at Him and
Him alone—that is precisely what true, evangelical confession calls out to us to do.

The fact remains: "Your sins are forgiven." (Matthew
9:2.) Sins *are* forgiven! But this forgiveness must be effectu-
ated, dispensed, and imparted—all of which is done through
Christ. Christ has deposited His word of forgiveness in the
church. Christ does not remain off to Himself; He gathers
about Him a people in whose midst He does His work. To
be sure, He is the sole source of forgiveness. It is He from
whose "heart shall flow rivers of living water." (John 7:38.)
Correctly interpreted this passage applies to Christ, and
may be read as follows: "He who believes in me, as the
scripture has said, 'Out of his heart shall flow rivers of
living water' "—namely, out of the heart of Christ. But immediately following we read that Christ was speaking
"about the Spirit, which those who believed in him were to
receive." (John 7:39.) Here the church is meant. Thus the
church now becomes His body, whose head He is, and in
the church there consequently flow the rivers of forgiveness.
We must not understand this to mean that Christ steps back
behind the church; rather He comes to the fore in His
church. Forgiveness takes place in the Holy Spirit, but the
Holy Spirit is the Lord Himself, living and present among

His own. Thus when there is forgiveness in and through the church, it is Christ Himself who forgives. That the church could pronounce the word of forgiveness through her own power is neither said nor implied. There can be forgiveness only in the authority of Christ. Christ has spoken the word of forgiveness; His witnesses, the apostles, receive it and pass it on. In the proclamation of His word the church repeats it after the apostles, and the word of forgiveness becomes efficacious among those who say it and among those who hear it.

This is what Christ ordered, promised, and commanded when He said to His disciples: "Receive the Holy Spirit. If you forgive the sins of any, they are forgiven; if you retain the sins of any, they are retained." (John 20:22-23.) And further: "Truly, I say to you, whatever you bind on earth shall be bound in heaven, and whatever you loose on earth shall be loosed in heaven." (Matthew 18:18.) And Jesus spoke to the whole church when He said to Peter: "I will give you the keys of the kingdom of heaven, and whatever you bind on earth shall be bound in heaven, and whatever you loose on earth shall be loosed in heaven." (Matthew 16:19.) Thus Jesus deposits the word of forgiveness in His church in order constantly to carry out forgiveness in the church. However, whoever desires and hungers for forgiveness comes to Him, to Christ. And whoever comes to Christ will not be cast out. (John 6:37.) Conversely, whoever passes the church by, passes Christ by and will not be freed from his sin. He continues to be bound; indeed, he becomes even more firmly bound than before. In *this* way the church becomes the place of final decision, and in *this* way the "keys of the kingdom of heaven" are handed over to the church.

The Catholic Church has used these three statements of

Christ to establish control over confession and penance. However, the Catholic Church was able to establish control only by misinterpreting and misusing Christ's words.

First of all, we must observe that confession in the Catholic Church takes place only in the *confessional* and thus becomes *private confession*. And, as we have already established, private confession in the confessional is confession before and directed toward the priest who forgives sins as a representative of Christ. Confession before Christ alone is no longer the question. Nor is consideration taken of the church to which Christ has given the keys of the kingdom and which He has established as the place from which forgiveness proceeds. Yet this is precisely what is meant by the words of Christ quoted above; Christ was not speaking of confession before a priest. Confession is the *work of the church* and is directed to *Christ* in the Holy Spirit.

But what does this mean? How are acknowledgment of sins and forgiveness—that is, confession—the work of the church? Christ has established three places in the church at which His word of forgiveness is issued and its power proven: *baptism, preaching,* as the place of proclamation, and the *communion table.* Wherever these places are provided, pure and genuine as our fathers expressed it, the church exists in which Christ will be present. These three places! The confessional is not included! Even though Luther may have retained the confessional, nonetheless he certainly did not do so in the sense of the Catholic Church. And we members of the evangelical church have no commission to establish it anew in any form. At the confessional our paths part from the Roman Church.

Baptism was instituted by Christ as the salutary sign that our lives from the beginning on, from the very first, are once and for all placed under His word of forgiveness. *Preaching* was ordained by Christ because the word of His witnesses is constantly to be communicated as His own. And He has the *communion table* in order again and again to encounter His people with the signs of His body and blood. There, at these three places, forgiveness and the disclosure of sin take place, but this is disclosure through Christ, not through us or through investigation of one's conscience by a priest; rather it is disclosure in, with, and under the forgiveness of Christ in His Word. This confession, the true confession and penitence, is wholly surrounded and permeated by the grace of Christ to the exclusion of any works of man. To be sure, human words do exist, the words of the witnesses in the Holy Scripture and the words of those who explain and communicate this witness, but they exist in such a fashion that it is Christ's own Word which comes to us in, with, and by these words. Of course we do have the *acknowledgment of sin*, but as an answer of the church to the Word which has been proclaimed to her. There is one thing above all: *the church prays*, she speaks to her Lord because He has spoken to her. We enter into *communion*, that is, into association with Him who calls the church to Himself in His Word and with the signs of holy deeds. Not only do we pray with words; we also pray in song, primarily in the songs of our fathers, in which love for Christ breaks forth powerfully in the church anew. In a word: *The worship service of the church* becomes the site of true, evangelical confession. Through the hearing of preaching, the taking of communion, and the practice of baptism, there is no worship service and no celebration of the Lord's Supper in which sins are not acknowledged and laid before Christ, and forgiven by Him! What else is it that we do when we pray the Lord's Prayer and make the "public confession of sins"? How should such prayer not be confession? And of course it scarcely needs to be emphasized that in her daily life the church continues this worship through reading the Bible, through prayer, and through her deeds. Thus the miracle of grace constantly occurs in the church.

In addition, when the right hour comes there will also be *private confession* before a neighbor or a brother or sister in the church. But this happens in the same way a miracle of grace takes place; it cannot be required and organized, it cannot become an institution subordinate to the injunction of a priest. We call it *ministry* when "one confesses his sin to the other." Such ministry, not only practiced by the pastor (however much this is especially his task) but also and primarily reciprocated among church members, is a sign of life which must not be absent from the church. We shall have more to say of this later.

Do the acknowledgment of sins and the assurance of grace in the Catholic Church take place only in the confessional? Are not sins also admitted and words of grace said in the liturgy of the Catholic Mass? But who is it who reads the liturgy in the Catholic Mass? Who prays? Again it is the priest and the priest alone who as the representative of Christ presents the sacrifice of the Mass at the altar of His church. He then offers his prayer by virtue of this his priestly authority, the authority by which he then forgives sins in the confessional. The Mass and confession are most intimately linked. Both are based on an authority which is a usurpation of the sole authority of Christ. That alone is sufficient to make us deeply suspicious of the Catholic confession and to show it as something for which we have no longing whatever. There is only one thing which we constantly need to do: to be concerned for the resuscitation and building up of our church. This will be achieved through proper evangelical worship services, living preaching, and true prayer. Also we must not scorn baptism, and we must frequently and joyfully partake of the Lord's Supper. In addition there must be genuine, ministering, evangelical confession. Then there will flow among us the rivers of living water which proceed from the body of Christ which is the church.

But what do we mean by "genuine, ministering, *evangelical private confession*"? What is it? What do the fathers of our church, the Reformers, have to say about it? How does it differ from false, Catholic confession? Does it have a basis in the Holy Scripture?

Let us make one point straight off: In its essence, evangelical private confession is no different from the general confession of the congregation—both are concerned with the forgiveness of sins. In private as well as public confession, it is Christ who uncovers and forgives the sin and thereby builds His church. We call it individual or private confession because the call to forgiveness which is directed to everyone in the preaching, Holy Communion, and prayer of the congregation is now directed in particular to one single person.

Why is it directed to the individual? We shall answer with a quotation from Calvin: "Nor is private absolution less efficacious or beneficial, when it is requested by those who need a particular remedy for the relief of their infirmities. For it frequently happens, that he who hears the general promises, which are addressed to the whole congregation of believers, nevertheless remains in some suspense, and his mind is still disquieted with doubts of the forgiveness of his sins. The same person, if he discloses to his pastor the secret distress of his mind, and hears this language of the gospel particularly directed to him, 'Be of good cheer; thy sins be forgiven thee' will encourage his mind to an assurance, and will be liberated from that trepidation with which he was before disturbed." (*Institutio christianae religionis,* III/4,14.)* And in the basic document of the reformed faith, the statement is made: "We have no objection if someone who is oppressed by the burden of his sins and by unsettling temptations wishes to obtain advice, instruction and consolation privately from a servant of the church or from another brother who is well-grounded in the Word of God" (*Second Helvetian Confession,* Chapter XIV).

Both statements presuppose the general acknowledgment of sins as practiced in the worship service of the church. But there are people who are driven by deep-seated problems of guilt for whom the way to the word of forgiveness must be opened through such personal confession to a fellow man. Who of us has not already had this experience? It is on this basis that private confession is possible and right. Martin Luther, especially, upheld this sort of confession; from the distress of his own life he knew what it means when the word of forgiveness of Christ is addressed to us quite personally by a brother to whom we turn as our confessor. Luther writes: "Besides this useful, daily, and open confession there is also a confession which may take place privately between two brothers and if, from some special cause, we become disturbed with restless anxiety and find our faith insufficient, we can make our complaint to a brother in this

* This translation quoted from: John Calvin, *Institutes of the Christian Religion,* translated by John Allen, seventh American edition. Philadelphia: The Westminster Press.

private confession and obtain his advice, comfort and support whenever we desire. . . . Now wherever there is a heart which feels its sins and desires consolation, it has here an unfailing resource in the Word of God, that God through a human being releases and acquits it of sins." ("A Brief Admonition to Confession," in the *Larger Catechism*.) *

What is the difference between this evangelical private confession, as championed by the Reformers, and Catholic confession? First of all, we must bear in mind that the Catholic Church knows confession only in the form of *private confession to a priest*. And it was against precisely such confession that the great attack of the Reformers was directed. The Catholic Church knows nothing of a general and public confession in the worship service of the congregation. The fathers of our church established this general confession by the congregation in direct contrast to confession before a priest. Ministering confession, of which they also had knowledge, can only be practiced when confession by the congregation provides the background and basis. What a difference there is between this form of confession and confession before a priest!

In *evangelical confession*, in ministering confession, the authority to forgive sins rests entirely with Christ. The sole function of our fellow man, be he brother or sister (and why should confessions not also be heard by sisters in the church?), is to express the word of Christ which He has already spoken. And he who seeks confession needs only to listen to this word. If he listens to it, he is absolved. If he does not want to listen, he remains bound, he remains in his

* This translation quoted from: Martin Luther, *Smaller and Larger Catechism*, 2nd edition (Newmarket, Virginia, 1855).

disobedience. Even if the brother to whom I acknowledge my sin should dare say to me, "I absolve you," he would do so only on the basis of Christ's words. Even then his *"absolvo te"* ("I absolve you") is nothing other than the form of the word in which Christ Himself absolves. One man does not absolve another; it is Christ who absolves. For this reason it would be better for us not to use the expression *Absolvo te,* but rather to close the confession with a prayer and with the assurance, "Christ absolves you!" Those who wish to introduce confession as an institution in the evangelical church insist that the expression "I absolve you" be used as a fixed formula at every confession. But do they not see how closely they are approaching Roman confession to the priest?

In *Catholic confession* it is the *priest* who gives absolution by virtue of his ordination to the office of priest. Confession is a sacrament, that is to say, it is a divine institution which is administered by the church and laid in the hands of the priest. Christ assigns His authority to the priest, and for that reason the priest's *"absolvo te,"* his absolution, has direct, divine power. Thus his absolution is not to be interpreted "deprecatively," that is, it is not to be interpreted as a supplication to Christ [Cf. Matthias Joseph Scheeben, *Handbuch der katholischen Dogmatik* (*Handbook of Catholic Dogmatics*), §380.] What point would there be in supplication to Christ if the priest himself has authority to free us from sins directly? But such an idea is an encroachment on the free grace of Christ; indeed, it is more than that, it is an annulment of the grace of Christ!

In *evangelical confession* forgiveness is a *gift,* nothing but a gift. Man can do nothing to obtain it. He receives it. Nor is the acknowledgment of his sin a work which man does in order to acquire grace for himself. Forgiveness comes to him

without any merit on his part, and he admits his sin out of
remorse born of sheer gratitude. Christ could say to me: "I
am your judge! Away with you, I cannot use you!" But this
is precisely what He does not say; rather, He forgives!
What a strange judge! What an undeserved verdict!

How very different the situation is in *Catholic confession!*
Catholic confession is really a *legal proceeding,* corresponding to human jurisprudence on earth. The sinner must be
found guilty of his sins. He must enumerate them one by
one. He must show remorse and apply for a merciful verdict.
And the judge acts "as a magisterial person who has the
power to decide whether to condemn or absolve, according
to the circumstances." The priest must decide whether or
not the sinner can receive forgiveness "on the basis of the
state of the sinner's conscience and the law of Christ."
(Scheeben, *op.cit.*) Catholic confession is a matter of justification by works and not by grace alone. The acknowledgment of sins as a human work precedes forgiveness. And then
the confession is completed by the human work of penance
imposed by the priest. How sinister is this power of office
which is the property of the priest! But on the other hand,
some of those who would revive the institution of confession
in the evangelical church cannot emphasize strongly enough
the authority of office of the evangelical pastor and for this
reason insist that confession can be heard only by the pastor
by virtue of his office; under no circumstances will they
permit confession to be heard by any ordinary church member. Where will this overevaluation of the office of pastor
lead? Woe to all clericalism! Clericalism imperils the sole
validity of grace in that very church which professes to live
by grace alone.

Linked with the legalistic aspect of confession is the

coercive character found in the Catholic practice of confession. Evangelical confession rests entirely on the grace of Christ. One may confess as much as he wishes, but we have no jurisdiction over forgiveness. Confessing is a human act, and if Christ does not add grace our confessing is in vain, as are all our other actions. Because this is the case, confession is not to become an institution—nor can it be—by virtue of which forgiveness necessarily becomes obtainable. When confession takes place properly, it takes place in full freedom. It is subordinate to no law. In the Catholic Church, confession becomes a proceeding which can be regulated. The Church has control over grace, for it has taken the judgment of Christ into its own hands. The confessional bench becomes the judge's bench before which man must appear, and from which the deputy of Christ can remit sins or not. In the Catholic Church there is no way to forgiveness other than the Church's administration of confession understood in these terms. For this reason the Church does not merely offer confession; it orders confession, it compels man to confession.

The Reformation directed its assault against this coercive confession. Luther said: "In reference to confession, we have ever taught that it should be free, that the tyranny of the pope should be put down, and that we should be liberated from all his constraints and relieved of the intolerable burdens imposed on the Christian community. For hitherto, as we have all experienced, nothing has been more grievous than the compulsion of everyone to confession . . . and the consciences of men were tormented to such a degree with the enumeration of so many kinds of sins that no one could confess fully enough." ("A Brief Admonition to Confession,"

in the *Larger Catechism.*)* Forgiveness of sins is joyful
news because it is the news of God's free grace. In legalistic
coercive confession, grace is tied to the practice of confession which is manipulated by the church, and joy in being
forgiven is killed.

There is a last point: The priest who hears confession is
not only the judge who frees and binds; at the same time, he
is the "spiritual physician." (Scheeben, *op.cit.*) The body and
soul receive healing effects from confession. We shall not
contradict the statement that forgiveness of sins has healing
power. The word of forgiveness is a word of power. The
paralytic in the Gospel was not only absolved of his sins, he
was also healed. (Matthew 9:2-8.) The uplifting of the soul
brought about by proper confession can cause recovery from
melancholy and anguish, and recuperative powers can be
released even in the sphere of physical suffering. But it is
grace and grace alone when this happens. The priest is not
the physician—"The Lord is your physician"—and confession
is not a necessary prerequisite. These healing forces can
come upon sick spirits and bodies simply through hearing
the Word of God, or in prayer or at the communion table.
It is true that when a man really hears the word of forgiveness much can change in his life. The close connection between sickness and sin, between healing and forgiveness,
now becomes visible.

Does all this hold true for Catholic confession? Catholic
confession is fallible, and we are striving for a quite different
confession, for a confession which is true. But is not evangelical confession also a fallible human action time and time
again? Yet who is able, who wants to keep Christ from giv-

* Luther, *op. cit.*

ing His grace in a fallible human act? His grace is *free* grace, and the wind of His spirit blows when *He* wishes it.

Forgiveness causes healing. But one thing we must not do: We must not reach for forgiveness as we reach for medicine. The word of forgiveness is not a medicine which is at our disposal for use against injuries to the body and soul. Once and for all we must be warned against misusing confession as a means of grace. This abuse is not limited to the Catholic Church; we in the evangelical church are likewise guilty. The modern confession-movement is not free of it. We can have completely renounced the hierarchy of the priesthood and all coercive confession, but we are far from realizing that grace lies in the hand of Him alone who is able to give it and wishes to give it; we do not realize that it is not something which we can procure for ourselves. We go to church, we pray to our Father in heaven, we celebrate the Lord's Supper, and we confess, but we observe and use all this as a means, we make use of it as a method to procure for ourselves access to salvation and healing. We do not seek God Himself and His emancipating grace for His sake; rather, we want to requisition God for our sakes. We pursue aims which are no different from those of the Catholic who confesses or makes a pilgrimage. That Simon Magus who, as we read in the book of Acts (Acts 8:9-24), wanted to purchase the Holy Spirit in order to use Him as a healing power walks among us today in modern dress. Whoever longs for confession as an institution of healing is practicing pious self-help and is on the way to magic. It is not I who can help myself through my confessing; Christ helps, Christ Himself and Christ alone.

At this juncture we must concern ourselves with one last question: Is not the *process of confessing* significant and useful in itself, quite aside from Christ's act of grace which can take place in confession? Consider the fact that confession calls for an examination of conscience, a deep look into the spiritual life of a man, no matter what else may be involved. And such an examination can cause cleansing and clarification of sorts. When one man opens his heart to another, that in itself means help, it means being lifted out of inner loneliness, out of egocentricity, and out of a cramped state of mind. This cannot be denied or disregarded. After confessing, one is eased internally. Regarded along these lines—that is, aside from the word of forgiveness—confession is a psychotherapeutic process, a sort of cleansing treatment for the psyche. The man seeking confession becomes the patient, and the confessor actually does become the physician. Far-reaching psychological perception and highly significant psychotherapeutic counsel come into play. Ministry becomes psychotherapy in religious garb, and psychotherapy becomes a substitute for confession. For that reason the man whose soul is oppressed, the man who seeks help, will today perhaps no longer go to a priest or to a pastor, but rather to a physician. Modern psychiatry can be viewed to a large extent as a form of *secularized confession.*

And why not? We have no desire to challenge the amazing success of modern psychiatry; we rejoice in it. Whether or not he knows it, the physician is also in the service of God. And because the physician does assume therapy of psychological ills, the ministrant is directed once again to the quite different task with which he is charged. The healing of mental sickness, release from psychic constrictions, cleavages, and complexes in the sphere of the inner nature of man is one thing, but encounter with God, freeing man of guilt before Him, breaking the fetters of sin, and saving man from the power of darkness is something quite different. Modern medicine may make great achievements in healing, but medicine has not yet cured the sickness of sin so that the infirmities of body and soul are actually eliminated. This healing, healing from the affliction of sin, is the work of the grace of Christ and is what is involved in the forgiveness of sins through the communication of the Word of God to the church. Here is where living ministry has and will keep its place and its mission alongside and beyond all psychotherapy.

There are physicians who are aware of this ministering aspect in the practice of their profession. And there are even some physicians who summon a ministrant for their patients and who in a way act as ministrants themselves from time to time. Consequently we have no reason to distrust the medical profession or to regard it as competition. Sometimes psychotherapeutic treatment by a doctor can go beyond the search for healing and can open the way to a true awareness of sin and thus to inquiry and search for the salvation of forgiveness. Yes, if it is pleasing to God, the miracle of grace can also take place in the doctor's office. But since in any event it is grace which is involved, we must continue to have ministry, and there is one necessary ingredient which must never be omitted in and with our ministry: true, evangelical confession. We would be more than foolish if we no longer took seriously our task in the church as proclaimers of the word of forgiveness or if we should want to exchange this task for mere psychotherapy, however useful psychotherapy will be if we can have some knowledge and understanding of it. There still remains grace, and Christ continues to be the sole dispenser of grace. We are told this by the fathers of our church on the basis of their struggle against all false confessing. And we are also told this by the Holy Scripture, from which they acquired all their knowledge of Christ and of the freedom and power of His grace.

The Holy Scripture! In all our considerations thus far we have been guided by the Scriptures. If now in conclusion we closely examine what the Bible teaches of confession, we shall make the noteworthy discovery that confession and confessing take up but little space in the Bible itself—only so much as is allocated by God Himself. Let there be confessing, if through it He can emerge in His grace. However, He can also appear elsewhere, and without our human private confession. Thus our confession before men disappears in His presence, so that we perceive Him alone and allow Him to do His work. If only the revivers and advocates of private confession would read their Bibles more carefully! It is strange how weak and superficial is the Biblical justification for confession cited in present-day writing on the subject.

We have already discussed the *three main places* in which Christ Himself transfers the word of forgiveness to His church. It has become clear to us that the establishment of private confession is not involved at any of these three places, particularly confession before the priest as practiced in the Catholic Church. Rather, the church, represented by the apostles, becomes the place where sins are remitted or not; however, this is done in the Holy Spirit, and that means through Christ Himself and through His Word.

How does the church become the place where sins are remitted? This comes about through the *prayers* of the church. The Lord of the church is called, and He steps forth as one who hears these prayers. In the first place, we sing

Psalms. "Oh thou who hearest prayer! To thee shall all flesh come on account of sins. When our transgressions prevail over us, thou dost forgive them." (Psalm 65:2-3.) Because the church has a Lord who hears prayers, she calls to Him and does not cry in vain. The Psalms are in the Old Testament, but the New Testament church gathers them up as their prayers. Through Christ the church has knowledge of the activity of God who bends down to us. Like a physician who lays his ear on the breast of the critically ill patient in order to hear the heartbeat, so God places His ear to the earth to hear the softest sigh which rises up from the mouth of man. In addition, look at Psalms 32 and 51, to name only these two, with their cries for forgiveness. What do we hear in these Psalms—instructions to confess before man? By no means! Again we hear a prayer to the Lord our God, and His promise: "For day and night thy hand was heavy upon me . . . I acknowledged my sin to thee, and I did not hide my iniquity; I said, 'I will confess my transgressions to the LORD'; then thou didst forgive the guilt of my sin." (Psalm 32:4-5.)

But does not confession form a background for Psalm 51, the *confession of David?* (2 Samuel 12:1-14.) Let us carefully examine what actually happened. To be sure, the sin of David was disclosed through a man, the prophet Nathan. But in what way was his sin disclosed? Did David have to confess to Nathan? By no means! This was a case of the direct intervention of God. The sinner did not seek out a father confessor; rather, the prophet appeared and immediately said to David: "You are the man!" You have sinned! You have done it secretly, but God has seen it and will bring it to light. David did not recognize and acknowledge his sin on his own initiative as would have to be done in regular confession. Only after Nathan's words was David able to make his confession. And then, just as surprisingly as the disclosure of his sin, there came forgiveness. "David said to Nathan, 'I have sinned against the LORD.' And Nathan said to David, 'The LORD also has put away your sin.'" (2 Samuel 12:13.) And so Psalm 51 is the subsequent prayer of penitence of him whose sin had already been forgiven; it is nothing other than thanks and praise for forgiveness. Is this not the opposite of our concept of confession? Certainly this passage cannot be used to introduce an evangelical imitation of the Catholic practice of confession. In the case of David, God alone acted through His prophet. This was one lone incident, and no mention is made of an institution, or method, or way of salvation which we are instructed to follow.

The situation is no different in the New Testament. Here, too, we see the free, sovereign acts of God in Christ. John the Baptist rose up and preached repentance. (Matthew 3, and parallels.) But essentially, repentance was not at all the first point which he made in his preaching. The proclamation of the gracious act of God who in His Son establishes His Kingdom and in such a way that He comes to us sinners in baptism—this is what John the Baptist preached. Now of course this means repentance, but this repentance can be compared to a sick man who rises from his bed because health has been given him. He does not become healthy because he arises, he arises because health has been given him. We acknowledge our sins and are moved to repent because the Kingdom of God draws near; it is not the other way around. We can express this another way: The action of God comes first. The promise of the Kingdom of God is the beginning; it is not the confession of sins which comes first.

In the light of the new day which then dawns, our sins are
revealed. And thus confession—if we may use the word here
—has this meaning: the uncovering of sin in the light of forgiveness which comes through "the Lamb of God, who takes
away the sin of the world," as John the Baptist expressed it.
(John 1:29.) We go about confession in the wrong order:
First comes urgent talk of sin, then there is to be a change
of ways which we ourselves are to effect, and finally there
comes the assurance of forgiveness. Our practice of confession lacks as first element the dawning of the radiant light of
forgiveness. It also lacks the revelatory and prophetic elements. Our practice of confession consists of miserable,
human, legalistic efforts; we act as though confession were
a matter of methodology, rather than a divine act.

Let us now consider Matthew 18:15-20, a passage re-
peatedly cited in instructions on confession by those in our
church as well as by Roman Catholics. Does this passage
not command us to practice private confession before our
fellow men? But here, too, no mention is made of a deputy
who, so to speak, rises up because of his office to hear confession. Here as well it is the Lord Himself who in His
church deals with sinners; He is "in the midst of them."
(Verse 20.) The men mentioned in this passage go before
their brother to "tell him his fault." But again it is not their
task to bring their brother to the point of acknowledging his
sins before them. Rather they make his sins known to him in
the name of the Lord. It is not they who judge, it is the
Lord. It is also not up to them to forgive. Their brother is to
return to the church, where the word of forgiveness of the
Lord quite certainly awaits him. According to our rules of
confession the sinner is to acknowledge his sins, that is, he
is to state them. But in this passage the sinner is told his sin,

and the decision is made from above. Either he listens to the Word of the Lord in the church—and this is a constant miracle—or he stays away and his sin is retained. And this again is an act of the Lord. So that this may not happen, the witnesses of the church speak to him of his sin as Nathan spoke to David. We see that the act of confession as usually understood is not treated by this passage either. Here as well, the action of the Lord is the all-embracing, into which the sinner is drawn.

James 5:14-18 should also be discussed, since it is frequently cited by those favoring private confession: "Therefore confess your sins to one another." And indeed, why should we not! But again our confessing should be an event within the framework of the church, so that here as well the power of forgiveness of the Lord of the church is presupposed. Forgiveness does not take place simply because we have already confessed; rather we confess our sins to each other in the church because forgiveness already exists and because forgiveness is the help which alone helps. One thing we must not overlook in considering this selection from the book of James: The passage is not primarily concerned with forgiveness, but with the healing of the sick. Sickness may and is to be healed in the church. Sin is mentioned here because sin is the root of sickness. Acknowledgment of sins in the church, and thus within the area of forgiveness, opens the way for healing, inasmuch as the way becomes free for prayer through the acknowledgment of sin. Healing takes place through the "prayer of a righteous man," that is, of a man whose sins are forgiven. Here we see that mysterious connection between sickness and sin, between prayer for forgiveness and healing. But neither prayer nor the acknowledgment of sins is viewed here as means which we could

employ to be healed; rather the Lord of the church acts
miraculously upon sin-sick men and includes them—includes us sin-sick men—in His actions. We are not dealing
with a system or institution, or with a gateway which we
could use as an entrance to the inner reaches of the divine
act; admitting our sins to each other will not bring that
about. Divine grace is what comes upon us. Nothing would
be more perverted than to create from divine grace a practice of confession which could enable us to attain forgiveness and healing. Forgiveness and healing take place when
it pleases Christ to prove Himself to us as Saviour. And He
wants to do this! This is precisely what is told to us in this
portion of the book of James, and we are permitted to hear
this truth and pass it on. Know Him and pray to Him, and
then He Himself will open the way to repentance and to
healing! This is the promise and the command which are
given to us here.

There is another passage which deals with the reciprocal
acknowledgment of sins. In Matthew 5:23-25, Jesus tells His
disciples first to be "reconciled to your brother" who "has
something against you" when going to the altar—the altar of
course means the place of forgiveness. But note: The brother
is the "accuser" who wants to accuse me. It is not I who
have something against him, he has something for which to
reproach me. He is angry with me, I am not angry with him.
And now I (not this my accuser!) am to seek reconciliation.
In our acknowledging of sins and confessing we do the very
opposite; we profess as our transgression the anger which
burns in us against the other person, while in Christ's statement the animosity which another has against me is considered to be a trespass for which I must seek reconciliation.
And I am not to seek reconciliation by making confession

before a third party; I must go to my accuser and reconcile myself with him. This is the way Jesus views "confessing our sins to one another." What a strange confession! This passage is in the Sermon on the Mount, and the Sermon on the Mount proclaims the breaking through of the Kingdom. This means that such reconciling, such confessing to one another, takes place in the light of the new life which dawns with Jesus. Once again it is the working of His grace when it happens.

Let us now consider how Jesus called His disciples to walk in His steps and made them messengers of His grace. Did He in any place demand confession as a prerequisite for His call to them? Of course in Luke 5:1-10 we read the account of how Peter met Jesus and broke out with the words: "I am a sinful man." But he did not recount his sins, and Jesus did not administer absolution to him. In this passage the main emphasis is placed on the miracle of the large haul of fish. Jesus revealed Himself to Peter as the Lord of creation, and in light of this self-revelation of the Lord it became clear that Peter simply could not hold back in the presence of this Lord. At the same moment it also became clear (and without an explicit confession) that despite his unworthiness and although Peter must fear Jesus, he nonetheless belonged to Jesus and was accepted by Him. Of course this might be called an act of confession, but how very different it is from our practice.

Always it is Jesus who uncovers the sin in order to wipe it out. This is what happened to the Samaritan woman at Jacob's well. (John 4:6-29.) The penetrating eye of Jesus saw what she was before she could lay open her life to Him. And at the same moment He revealed Himself to her as the ambassador of God. The same was true with the

adulteress whose disgrace the scribes brought before Him.
She, too, did not confess before Him, but He forgave her
and changed her life. (John 8:1-11.) Forgiveness radiates
from Him, and sin cannot exist in the face of this forgiveness; sin is uncovered and taken away without any action on
the part of the sinner. That is the other thing, the new thing,
about the act of confession, if one still insists on using the
term.

In another aspect as well, our concept of confession differs
from the practice of Jesus. Jesus imposed no particular
works of penance on those whom He forgave; He imposed
no reparations which would have to be made. However, He
transformed their lives, He placed them on the new path of
obedience, perhaps with the few words "Go, and do not sin
again" (John 8:11), sometimes even without words. In and
with forgiveness there comes over men a transformation and
change. In and with grace the command is present, but not
as a law which is imposed upon us: "For my yoke is easy,
and my burden is light." (Matthew 11:30.) His command is
full of life which comes upon us from eternity. He gives His
people "power to become children of God." (John 1:12.)
Of course there will be changes in our lives, and we will do
works of repentance born of gratitude, but these are works
of grace which He performs upon us. The sequence which
we observe with Jesus is not the sequence which we observe
in our confessing: first the law and only then the evangel.
The sequence is rather: first the evangel and then obedience,
but obedience caused by Him.

Let us now summarize our discussion. Confession, when
examined from a Biblical point of view, is quite different
from our concept and practice. Confession is genuine when

it comes entirely from the grace of Christ and is illuminated by grace. To confess to one another means to meet one another in this grace. Thus confession can be nothing which is planned by man; we cannot demand it of each other, and we can force no one to confess. Confession is a happening which Christ sends.

This means, however, that true confession takes place within the church—let this be re-emphasized. *The church of Jesus must be present* as the place where we receive the word of forgiveness. In, with, and through the issuance of this word comes the miracle of the uncovering and taking away of our sin: our guilt is extirpated, we are freed from the domination of sin, and a new life is awakened. Whoever, like Peter, is fearful before Christ can be accepted and transformed by Him. But because this takes place again and again in ministering conversation with our neighbor, there is such a thing as confession—as a matter of fact, in the form of a conversation in which one person admits to another his sin before Christ.

Because this is the nature of confession it cannot be organized. We go to a neighbor to confide in him because God's Spirit is leading us. We then request that our neighbor grant to us the words of grace, and he does so. Thus we confess without law or compulsion.

It is not necessarily the pastor to whom we go. But it can be, and frequently is, the pastor. The existence of a church with a pastor who is commissioned to minister and is thus prepared to hear confession is a sign that grace is present and that it waits for us. To be sure, such ministry is no easy matter; it is a narrow path from which one can fall at every step. Ministry is not practiced through the awareness of one's office. There must be humility, a trait which is strong

and also rare. The ministrant must constantly keep in mind
that there are no methods or tricks which he can employ
to proceed safely. We may build confessionals as was done
at the church assembly in Frankfurt, but the forgiveness of
sins cannot be installed. The ministrant is like the man mentioned in the Sermon on the Mount. (Matthew 5:41.) In
order to show the way to the broad expanse of grace, he will
go not merely one, but two or perhaps ten miles into the
depths of an entangled life if he is asked. Humility, de-
votion to one's neighbor, real encounter with him, and then
total reliance on grace do not preclude the need for certain
abilities and gifts, and even training. We must above all
have training in the Holy Scripture which alone teaches
what true ministry is. The ministrant must also have the gift
and ability to understand men; that is, he must know
human nature, and training in psychology can be of real
service. But on the other hand, of what value are all so-called
talents and training in ministering? They can give us a false
sense of security if we do not have a heart which listens to
God. Let us respect psychology, but it is nothing in ministering without the prayer of faith, because it is nothing without
the miracle of grace which comes upon us and for which we
can only make supplication. The true ministrant is the ministrant who has been blessed.

Once more let it be repeated: The ministrant does not at
all need to be a clergyman. Part of the freedom of grace consists of the fact that Christ sends to us just any brother or
sister in the church, any of the lowest, or someone whom we
do not know and have not summoned. This person comes to
us without any set appointment or office hours, and through
him we come into that discussion of grace which we need.

The hour of confession can be at an unexpected time, and the person to whom we admit our sin can be present accidentally, unexpectedly, and unsought. Also the *site of such confession* is not prescribed. It does not have to be a confessional, a vestry, or a church room. There is just as little need for candles or a crucifix as for a book with a special liturgy for the confession. All such things are more obstructive than beneficial, because they give the appearance of organized confession. Genuine, ministering confession can take place in any living room, bedroom, or kitchen, on the train, or during a walk, just as well as in the study of the pastor or in a church room. It is all a matter of grace, and grace is not tied to a set location or practice—and most definitely not to a printed liturgy. Grace is free, over against all these things. And when grace does emanate in a liturgical form, it is not because of the liturgy. Grace occurs—and let this once more be emphasized—just as miracles occur. And miracles cannot be brought about or even replaced by human measures, however solemn they may be.

But are there not some people who are particularly *gifted* ministrants? If there are such ministrants, they themselves do not know of their so-called gift. Men who know, or think they know, that they are gifted do not have this gift at all. What is meant by the word "gifted"? Certainly only one thing is meant: called and pardoned by Christ. And no one is guaranteed such pardon by virtue of his office and for his whole life long, the period for which the Catholic priest is ordained. Pardon must be given each time anew, in each individual conversation. It is an event, not an institution; without it ministry becomes routine, and routine is the opposite of calling. Consequently, ministrants who have been thus blessed are always outsiders and do not conduct themselves as officials and according to rules. The two Blumhardts were such men, not so much "gifted" as they were ministrants and confessors constantly filled with grace, and for that reason the official church and its officeholders looked at them askance. And in the Catholic Church we find that strange contemporary of the elder Blumhardt, Jean Baptiste de Vianney, the curé d'Ars, known to us from the novels of Bernanos. Characteristic of its freedom, grace can be effective over and beyond the limits of church denominations and thus can be present in the confessional of the Church of Rome—as was the case with the curé d'Ars. To be sure, this truth certainly does not justify the Catholic practice of confession; grace is effective in spite of their practice. But it does show us that Christ bows to no rule of confession and thus that even in false confession He can show Himself to be who He is. This fact can strengthen and comfort us ordinary ministrants not equipped with special gifts; it can strengthen and comfort every ordinary pastor or layman who practices the ministry of forgiveness on tormented consciences. For why should not the simple footsoldier of Christ be granted the miracle of grace?

But do there not also exist special *places of grace?* Unsought, they come into being where blessed ministrants are to be found. Men seeking spiritual help search out the abodes of these ministrants just as thirsty men look for an oasis. I could mention names. At the time of the two Blumhardts, *Bad Boll* was such an oasis. But these places become submerged and disappear, because grace does not tie itself to the dwellings of such ministrants any more than to any other set place. There is no such thing as an evangelical Lourdes! So far as the history of religion is concerned and also perhaps from a medical point of view, what happens in Lourdes may be extremely important; let us not mistake its significance. But "places of grace" which make use of the name of the Mother of God and which celebrate centennials are no real places of grace for us. However, there are real places of grace even today. And we are not thinking of those much-vaunted sites where with great propaganda revivals are set in motion, places which remind us more of Lourdes than of evangelical places of grace. Rather we are thinking of hidden and quiet spots. For some it is perhaps *Taizé* or *Grandchamp* where evangelical brotherhoods and sisterhoods gather in prayer and in service to their neighbor. For others it is a place such as the Swiss *Braunwald* where there is also a sisterhood which prays and serves and where the work of a ministrant and interpreter of the Bible (Pastor G. Spörri) has far-reaching effects. It is well for the church and the world that there are such places! God grants them to us as signs of His free grace.

Let one thing, however, be said in conclusion. The true place of grace can be, and time and time again will be, the *church*. Grace proceeds from the church, even from a poor and insignificant church. For this reason any true, evangelical confession must constantly lead to the church. We believe we have shown why this is so. And when we use the word "church" we are not afraid to think of that specific local congregation near our home. Even though the church may be poorly off in a world which, according to some, has changed, nonetheless the world has not changed so much that the church is superfluous. And even though the present pastor of the church is a weak man, still there is a promise for every worship service which is held and for all minister-

ing which is done. Even the light of a miserable congregation shines before God. And when we hold to the church
and pray for her, a fountain of grace can spring up in her
unexpectedly. Christ is and remains the Lord of the church.
And He does come in all the power and glory of His free
grace.

Essay Three

THE LORD'S SUPPER
IN THE LOCAL
CONGREGATION

Walter Lüthi

The Plight of the Lord's Supper

WE CANNOT PROPERLY SPEAK of the Lord's Supper in the local congregation without a detailed discussion of its *plight,* for certainly the Lord's Supper is rather generally in distress. If we go into this problem more closely, we must keep clearly in mind that it is quite easy to be ambiguous and imprecise in discussing the subject in general terms. Our church members often speak of the plight of the Lord's Supper with a vague feeling of discomfort but are unable to indicate clearly the nature of the difficulty. Laments have been voiced which are out of place and, indeed, really quite unfortunate. Many measures and steps have been sought and recommended to overcome the plight in which the Lord's Supper finds itself. Let us see to it, however, that they are fit and appropriate, for intolerable attempts have not infrequently been made to remedy the situation. There are even "difficulties" involving the Lord's Supper which, on closer examination, do not prove to be troubles at all. For example, it is quite questionable, as we shall see later, whether poor attendance at the Lord's Supper must automatically be considered a difficulty. In any event, "mass flocking to the eucharist" would by no means guarantee elimination of the problems.

In his work *Das Abendmahl im Neuen Testament* ("The Lord's Supper in the New Testament"), E. Gaugler points to the problematical elements involved in what church circles have been grouping for the past few decades under the slogan "The Plight of the Lord's Supper" (p. 3). Karl von Greyerz also treats the same subject in his decennial report on the Evangelical-reformed Church of the canton of Bern, Switzerland. He writes in part: "We may be very certain that the present-day avoidance of and flight from the Lord's Supper has deeper roots than can be eliminated by external measures such as individual cups, nonalcoholic wine, seated communion, more frequent celebration, and saying a Bible verse to each communicant" (p. 80).

We are very much in agreement with von Greyerz when he lays his finger on a sore spot on the body of the evangelical church: "The Lord's Supper, which we claim to be a commemoration by the congregation, begins just as half of the congregation—and in some places, almost the whole congregation—has left, and thus it becomes an appendage in the empty church. One way or the other we must change this unworthy and unevangelical situation which can be seen in churches everywhere. The officials of the church should seriously consider how this situation can best be changed" (p. 81). Certainly the struggle against this plight of the Lord's Supper is deserving of "serious consideration." However, in order to avoid disastrous fallacies and want of clarity in this struggle, the necessity of which no active church member or conscientious elder will doubt, we should like to suggest a distinction which can be drawn.

Much confusion and harm can be avoided if we realize that there are two types of difficulties or problems with the Lord's Supper. There are difficulties which are rooted in the nature of communion itself, and there are those which are caused by the congregation. We should be careful to distinguish between these two types. The difficulties inherent in the Lord's Supper must be borne and affirmed by the congregation, and any counteracting measures or attempts would not only be foolish and preposterous, they would also be nothing short of abominable. On the other hand, the difficulties for which the congregation itself is responsible must be overcome if possible, but with appropriate measures. Any church failing to consider corrective measures will be persisting in a wrongdoing. Legitimate difficulties which stem from the Lord's Supper itself are not without God's promise; however, we can plead no promise for the difficulties which we ourselves have caused.

The legitimate difficulties could also be called the offense of the Lord's Supper, in the sense that we speak of the offense of the cross in our Christian teachings. We must pay close heed to this aspect of offense in the Lord's Supper, especially in the world of today. God be thanked that in recent years there have been clearer and clearer signs that an overcoming of the difficulties mentioned above has been in process within the evangelical church. Deepened, theological, Biblically oriented work is being carried on by men concerned primarily with a more Biblical understanding of the nature of the sacraments. We do not go too far when we speak of the actual joy of discovery now being felt. Despite —indeed, because of—this joy of discovery which is only too understandable in view of the existing difficulties, we must be careful that we do not reach for the recovered treasures too gaily and massively, and that we do not begin to make use of them too self-confidently. We must keep in mind that there is offense in the Lord's Supper, and we can alleviate or resolve it just as little as we can the offense of the cross. Later we shall try to show more clearly what is meant by this statement.

In the next five sections of this essay we shall deal with the difficulties which are caused by the Lord's Supper itself, and in the last six we shall examine the type of difficulty for which the congregation is responsible.

The Offense of the Lord's Supper

A serious and extremely active church member once asked with a certain disquietude: Why is the Lord's Supper necessary along with and in addition to the word of forgiveness and of eternal life? He was glad and willing to hear the proclamation of the word of forgiveness of sins and the assurance of eternal life, but that was sufficient for him. In his opinion and according to his own personal experience, nothing else was needed. And, in fact, this man did attend preaching services rather regularly, but he never appeared at the table of the Lord.

In his report on the church of Bern, which we have already mentioned, Karl von Greyerz makes a similar observation when he quotes the moan of one pastor "that even regular attenders at preaching services never come to the Lord's Supper and openly admit that it means nothing to them; others do not express this idea, but think it. Explanation is of little value" (p. 81). The number of church members is actually not small who see in the Lord's Supper— with apologies for the expression—a sort of appendix in the body of the Christian church; they cannot really see why it exists, know only that it can be a burden, and thus think that it would be good and advisable to remove it by surgery. The fact that we are not only to hear but are also to "taste and see" (Psalm 34:8), indeed, eat and drink the forgive-

ness of sins and the assurance of eternal life—that is, that
we are to go to church not only with our ears but also with
our eyes and hands, with mouth and stomach—all of this is
a great offense to the evangelical Christian, but we must
bear and affirm it. And the offense is intensified by the fact
that we do not even know why the Lord of the church did
not stop with the Word.

What can we say about this problem? Certainly the Word
could have sufficed. But if Christ added the sacrament to the
Word—and not merely as an incidental addition or a bur-
densome appendage, but rather as a necessary center and
basis of His church along with the Word—then this is what
He did, and He is not obliged to render to us an account of
His reason. We must reconcile ourselves to the fact that
Jesus certainly knew why He left to us both the Word and
the sacrament, not the Word alone. Even though we do
not see the reason, we may have confidence that He does see
it. Our subjective opinion is not the standard of whether and
why the sacrament is necessary and useful, rather it is the
Lord's opinion which is the standard. When questioned on
the desirability and necessity of the holy Lord's Supper, we
can make absolutely no answer other than quite simply refer to the simple fact that Christ has established the Lord's
Supper and that whoever thinks he must reject it is rejecting
something of which Christ is the founder. And even if I do
not see what I would lose if I should stay away from the
table of the Lord, I must nonetheless keep clearly in mind
that I would be rejecting something which, in Christ's
thinking, is needed by the church. Whoever thinks that he
will cope with the offense of the sacrament by staying away
from the Lord's Supper for such purely personal feelings
and considerations must take into consideration that one day

people can stay away from every activity of the church for the same sort of subjective reasons. People would no longer see why they could not also be Christians without the church. It is very questionable whether a church member who thinks this way has ever realized what the church is, no matter how active he may be in the congregation. If we place subjective feeling above the Bible, what will keep us from finally rejecting the fact that out of all the countless possibilities for our salvation God chose that His Son should become flesh and die on the cross? From a human point of view, this is no more easily explainable than the institution of the Lord's Supper. Even if we know not one thing more about Christ's intention in establishing the Lord's Supper, the following point will be sufficient for us if we give it serious thought: Christ instituted the Lord's Supper for our salvation and because He loves us.

The Necessity of Faith

Let us first make a general observation. We cannot discuss the Lord's Supper without ceaselessly speaking of its great loftiness and splendor, but in the same breath we cannot avoid speaking of its great lowliness and simplicity. From the juxtaposition, indeed from the interweaving of loftiness and lowliness, there come some difficulties and offenses which will be considered in this and the next three sections.

We have the message, splendid beyond all supplication and understanding, that Christ the crucified offers Himself to His church in the Lord's Supper; He offers His body and blood, He offers Himself "bodily." There is a special power of life and deliverance in this bodily offer of salvation, in this tangible transmission of the highest possessions, in this bodily *communio* of Christ with us men, and this power proves to be a force and blessing of a special sort, especially to the most miserable among church members. Experience with the Lord's Supper in the congregation shows that people who see themselves threatened in their inner existence, people at the zero-point and Christians who feel an ax chopping at their roots, can be particularly receptive to the Lord's Supper and thankful that there exists a place where one can "taste and see that the LORD is good"! (Psalm 34:8.) Collapses of all sorts can cause a church member all of a sudden to begin to discover the Lord's Supper—this strange site of tactile and edible salvation. We notice that the Lord's Supper has become a great and priceless blessing for many church members who are inclined to be melancholy. Christians for whom the first beatitude has real meaning and who have looked down into the abyss of the possibility of their own rejection seem to have ears especially quick of hearing whenever the invitation to the table of the Lord is given. Also, there are Christians who find it difficult or impossible to hear the word of forgiveness for purely physical reasons. To this group belong not only those hard of hearing but also those who are dying or who are critically ill; many of these people extend their hands toward this strange concrete transmission of the message of salvation with a desire which is especially alive. Here, among those "who labor and are heavy-laden," there is refreshment of an especially splendid sort at the place where the fruits of the death of Christ—that is, the forgiveness of sin and eternal life—are eaten and drunk and where the hand is quite literally stretched out to Christ, just as Peter reached out as he sank into the sea.

There is a second factor involved, along with the great statement that forgiveness is tactile and edible: The Lord's Supper is not a form of eating and drinking which has the physical effect of other food, nor is the Lord's Supper ever a repetition of the sacrifice of Christ on the cross; rather, according to the express injunction of its Founder, it is the supper in memory of the sacrifice which was made one time and which is wholly sufficient for all time to come. The second part and continuation of the words of the Psalm, "Taste and see that the Lord is good," was translated by Luther: "Wohl dem, der auf ihn *trauet*" (Happy is the man who trusts in him). We see that Luther's translation was not without good reason. The Lord's Supper is an act of *faith;* however, it is not a matter of tasting and seeing, eating and drinking, which is dispensed to the recipients each according to his faith. The marvelously obvious and tangible aspect of the sacrament does not render faith unnecessary, rather it demands faith—a fact which is an offense and a difficulty in the Lord's Supper.

This difficult tension between faith and the obvious aspect of the Lord's Supper seems to be recorded most strikingly in the Gospel according to John, primarily in the sixth chapter which speaks in most graphic terms of the "eating of flesh" and "drinking of blood." However, the other aspect is mentioned in the same breath: "It is the spirit that gives life, the flesh is of no avail." Throughout this entire chapter the call and summons to faith is given with that urgency so noticeable with John. "Truly, truly, I say to you, he who believes has eternal life." (John 6:47.) And: "Every one who sees the Son and believes in him should have eternal life."

(John 6:40.) This offense of the necessity of faith is to be affirmed and borne as a difficulty in the Lord's Supper which is legitimate and desired by God. We should not interpolate any sort of arbitrary doctrine of transubstantiation in an attempt to mitigate or even solve this offense.

The following conversation held with a certain man trained in the natural sciences illustrates how sorely we are tempted to rid ourselves of this sort of difficulty in the Lord's Supper. The man in question had thrashed about in the materialistic waters of the modern natural sciences and was then in the process of seeking the way to the church. He was seeking in his own way, by looking about in the Roman Catholic and evangelical churches at the same time. In the course of the conversation it soon developed that the Mass, with its doctrine of transubstantiation, had a powerful attraction for him as a natural scientist and former materialist. He found something here which saved him from making a complete break with his previous way of thinking and which made Roman Catholic Christianity easier for him to accept than the evangelical teaching of the Lord's Supper. When he was told that he would take the body and blood of Christ by *faith alone,* he became almost violent. He declared his willingness to believe, but he did not want to receive the body and blood of Christ only by faith—he wanted to know. He wanted to take the body of Christ into his hand just as visibly and tactilly as any chemical compound in a test tube which he had analyzed and the composition of which he then knew. The mere assurance of salvation was not enough for him, he wanted a guarantee. The man became a Roman Catholic. The evangelical, Biblical bread of the Lord's Supper was not enough for him; he stretched out his hand for the "test tube," for the Host. We are sorely tempted to put aside and curb the difficulty of the Lord's Supper arising from the necessity of faith by interpolating a doctrine of transubstantiation—a concept foreign to the Bible. Receiving the Host brings about the guarantee of salvation; however, receiving the evangelical Lord's Supper effects the assurance of salvation through faith. As we know, the doctrine of the Mass goes so far that not even the presence of a congregation of believers is necessary. On the other hand, however, the congregation of believers is indispensable in the evangelical Lord's Supper.

The Grandeur and Poverty of the Lord's Supper

Christ promised that where Christians are gathered in His name He will be in the midst of them, and He further promised that He will be with His own until the end of the world. This is a grand declaration and a splendid promise which, to be sure, does not apply exclusively to the Lord's Supper but also to the hearing, praying, and singing congregation. Nonetheless we may lay claim to this promise in a special way for the Lord's Supper. Our claim is justified by the words of the Revelation of John: "Behold, I stand at the door and knock; if any one hears my voice and opens the door, I will come in to him and eat with him, and he with me." (Revelation 3:20.) The real presence of Him resurrected, together with all saints and angels, gives to the celebration of the Lord's Supper an unprecedented grandeur, of which the evangelical communicant has good right to be conscious. Even if there is no ringing of the bell and no dramatic genuflexion, nonetheless the evangelical Christian may approach the table of the Lord in awe—not as though he were stepping up to an ordinary table. We may and we must distinguish carefully between the body of the Lord and ordinary food and drink. We may draw near to the gracious presence of the resurrected One and may have ourselves drawn into the splendor of the victory of Easter—constantly knowing, however, that we cannot attend the distribution of the unspeakably rich prize of Easter as though it were an auction sale. Whoever goes to the table of the Lord draws near to the "throne of grace," in the incomparable words of the letter to the Hebrews; he draws near to the Lord and highest King. By and large we had rather see communicants take the bread and cup with an expression of timidity and a hand trembling with excitement than see people who, with their much too commonplace and casual gestures, perhaps have no emotion to hide because they are not conscious of the eventfulness of this encounter with the Lord to whom is given "all authority in heaven and on earth."

But let us immediately examine the Lord's Supper from the other perspective. Christ the high Lord is present at the Lord's Supper in poverty and in lowliness; He is present in the bread made by a baker in the congregation and in the wine delivered by a dealer who at the same time supplies the taverns in the area. The splendor arising from the presence of Him who has arisen stands in the sharpest contrast imaginable to what one actually sees with his eyes at the evangelical Lord's Supper. The Biblical, evangelical Lord's Supper is poor, humble, and meager in that which is apparent to the eye. This is an offense and difficulty in the Lord's Supper. The poverty and lowliness is manifested primarily by the extent of participation of the congregation at the table of the Lord. The fact that as a rule so few people come to the place where such a great Lord is present and can be met is and remains an incomprehensible offense. But we can bear this difficulty by keeping in mind that a paucity of communicants at the Lord's Supper can no more detract from its splendor in any respect than an extraordinarily large group could in any way increase its splendor. Much complaining about the plight of the Lord's Supper would be less dejected and lacking in faith if we realized that it is not the number of guests present at the Lord's Supper which gives content and value to the celebration, but rather that it is the presence of the one Guest, the real presence of Christ. Even though every pastor, church member, and elder understandably rejoices when there is a large number present, nonetheless if the attendance is poor they must never forget that we have been told that there is joy in heaven over every single sinner who repents. A single communicant is capable of setting all heaven in joyous excitement. And Christ is present where two or three are together in His name. There were no more than twelve at the first Lord's Supper, and one of those was a traitor. Thus, so far as the number of participants is concerned (even if this number should be in the thousands!), the Biblical, evangelical Lord's Supper has ever since its beginning resembled a pyramid—a pyramid which, however, has its broad and imposing base in eternity, in the invisible. Only the tiny tip of the pyramid towers up before our eyes as a sign, and no man can, on the face of it, tell that it is the tip of a heavenly pyramid. Only faith can withstand this offense of the poverty and lowliness of Christ in the Lord's Supper. Those of little or no faith, however, are ashamed of this poverty and disdain the lowliness of the Lord's table. Like the masters of this world they would like to see the broad base of the pyramid here on earth

—and if possible, in their own congregation—and are able to have full joy at the Lord's Supper only if the statistics seem favorable. They would like to demonstrate the power and greatness of the church through the presence of hundreds of thousands at the Lord's Supper. There are enough evangelical Christians who would like to ease this plight of the Lord's Supper by mass demonstrations. However, it is to be borne, and where it is borne in faith it has the promise which was given to the small but faithful group.

Christ in the Lord's Supper, Now and in the Future

Much lamenting about the plight of the Lord's Supper stems from the lack of attention given to the *tension* which exists between these two statements: "We are God's children now," and, "It does not yet appear what we shall be." (1 John 3:2.) This expression of the tension between faith in the present Lord and faith in the Lord of the future could be rephrased: We are now guests at the table of the Lord, but it does not yet appear what we shall be, we are not yet guests at the last supper, the great supper, the supper of those who have been perfected. This "not yet" places a damper on the beauty and splendor of the Lord's Supper—a point which we must consider bravely and courageously. And because of the "not yet" it is folly to try to make amends for the Lord's Supper by attempting with human, all too human, devices to give it the final "brilliance" which it now lacks. We are foolish to try to give to the Lord's Supper what it does not yet wish to have, by using candlelight and glittering robes, or by any sort of accentuated, mystic mood —in a word, through the use of aesthetics. Not until the last,

great Lord's Supper will a guest be removed who is not at-
tired in his Sunday finery. Of course, a simple Biblical liturgy
has a place in the celebration, but it is a perversion to try to
"fill and enrich" the Lord's Supper by an "enrichment of
the liturgy" and by making it a theatrical production. All
that we achieve through such human attempts at enrichment is merely to increase the solemnity. And if this is done
there is danger of enslaving the congregation under the
legalistic domination and constriction of stylized production and ritualistic correctness. By its nature, aesthetics dis-
penses a spirit of servility, and there is already more than
enough such legalistic solemnity in the way we conduct the
Lord's Supper all over the country. This sort of celebration
can be especially unbearable to young people. All honor to
aesthetics, but in the proper place. All other pleasures must
cease, even the aesthetic, when we partake of the holy
Lord's Supper. If we succumb to the great temptation to try
to transmit aesthetic pleasures to the congregation through
the Lord's Supper, we will bring about the result that, *mu-
tatis mutandis* (as in 1 Corinthians 11), some will be in-
toxicated and sated, but others, to whom these special
pleasures do not appeal, will suffer hunger so much the more
bitterly. Simple consideration for those who are not affected
by artistic pleasures should impose restraint on us so far as
all "communion culture" is concerned.

The fact that we can not yet have the Lord's Supper in
the brilliance of the last lights imposes upon the celebrating
congregation something roughly corresponding to fasting
during Advent. The congregation has to bear this damper on
its joy, rather than try to make the Lord's Supper liturgical
and aesthetic as a step in the opposite direction. However,
our fasting is to be free of all dismal looks. (Matthew 6:16-

18.) Never should sadness over the "not yet" become greater than joy over the "already now." Let this joy take its childlike course, for God gave us a childlike spirit, not a servile one, in order that we need not be afraid. Thus the communicant, looking into the past, may and should rejoice heartily and like a child at the salvation won for him on the cross and, as he looks into the future, he should rejoice at the promise of the last, splendid Lord's Supper in the return of Christ. This joy of the child of God is alien to all solemnity of the Lord's Supper which we ourselves have created and which is therefore so lethal. Joy loves the form of naturalness; it can be direct and it fears the printed program. The "exalting" of which we read in the Psalms or the "rejoicing" of the early Christian church at the Lord's Supper is scarcely imaginable at evangelical worship services, much less at communion services as we now celebrate them —except perhaps as a disturbance or scandal. This fact is to a large extent due to the rigidity resulting from our efforts to make the Lord's Supper an aesthetic occasion.

An incident several years ago reveals what can happen when there is a breakthrough of natural childlikeness. Hymn number 43 in our old hymnal was the solemn *Morgenglanz der Ewigkeit* ("Morning Radiance of Eternity") and number 42 was the happy *Die goldne Sonne* ("The Golden Sun"). One Easter Sunday when communion was to be celebrated the sexton erroneously posted hymn number 42 on the board instead of number 43. The organist noticed the error but because of the solemnity of the occasion did not dare call it to the attention of the minister. And so, toward the end of the service, she overcame her strong inhibitions and began to play hymn number 42. At first the congregation was taken aback by the cheerful tone but then began to sing hesitantly, "The golden sun, full of joy and delight." The song had the same effect as the opening of a window in a stuffy room. The singing of the congregation rose to an exaltation, and many members have not yet forgotten this Lord's Supper with the cheerful hymn.

The Lord's Supper as the Place of Existing and Ruptured Fellowship

The problem and offense of the Lord's Supper is especially apparent when we examine this sacrament from the point of view of fellowship among church members, as Paul does particularly in 1 Corinthians 11. Insofar as it represents fellowship with the Head, the Lord's Supper is also the fellowship of the members with one another. It is the sign and realization of brotherliness. It was no accident that the agapes (love feasts) of the early Christians were so closely connected with the Lord's Supper. (We shall discuss the agape later.) Cullmann reports that during the agape, the Christians often sang Psalm 133, which opens with the great words: "Behold, how good and pleasant it is when brothers dwell in unity." [Oscar Cullmann, *Urchristentum und Gottesdienst* (*Primitive Christianity and the Worship Service*), page 20, note 27.] Actually, the Lord's Supper is much more effective as a source of brotherliness in the congregation than we often imagine. Even the minister who is a none too industrious shepherd may sometimes see something of such real fellowship.

At first glance it may seem that Cullmann goes too far when he states that in early Christianity the sacraments early assumed the place of the New Testament miracles, but the fact of the matter is that any simple pastor or elder may even today see miracles while administering the bread and wine—the miracle of reconciliation and of brotherly fellowship. For example, a church member who has had a falling out with the minister, with perhaps the minister himself partly to blame, and who has stayed away from church life for years may come to the table of the Lord for the first time after the two have finally discussed the matter with each other. Or perhaps a married couple who have settled a conflict threatening to destroy their marriage come to the Lord's Supper together. Or a whole family in which there has been dissension between the parents and their adult children may come as a group to the table, thus allowing the minister to conclude that the bone of contention has been removed. As a servant at the table, can one help nodding encouragingly to a mother and her daughter-in-law when he knows that there has been tension between the two but now sees them coming, to eat from the same loaf and drink from the same cup! A minister may see a landlord at the table and know that he has quarreled with a renter. The minister waits with tense concern to see whether the renter will not also come up immediately. Just as his hopes are almost dashed, he sees the renter approaching among the last communicants and knows that now the battle is won. The sight of such miracles of reconciliation can make communion Sunday into a spiritual feast for the clergyman so that he, too, feels what the psalmist meant by the words: "A day in thy courts is better than a thousand elsewhere." (Psalm 84:10.)

But there is another side. It is precisely at the Lord's Supper that we feel the offense and difficulties, inasmuch as the Lord's Supper in the local church is not yet the perfected fellowship of the great Lord's Supper. The Lord's Supper is not merely revelatory of the fellowship which has been brought about among men; it can also reveal insufficient, or broken or even nonexistent human fellowship in the most painful and bitter way, so that the servant at the table has occasion to weep with the tearful as well as rejoice with the joyful. It is not unusual in an evangelical congregation today for a member finally to be forced into a divorce, despite the fact that he has resisted it as vigorously as possible and that it is against his Christian conviction. Then during the unwanted divorce proceedings, or possibly years later, the minister may see him coming to the Lord's table, perhaps holding back his tears only with difficulty, or even with tears suddenly streaming down his cheeks. In such cases the supper of the Lord becomes a sign not of fellowship which has been achieved, but rather of nonexistent or destroyed fellowship. In my observation, the number of persons is not small for whom the Lord's table in this way becomes the last, real, and sole refuge on earth. In my ministry I especially encourage all persons for whom the bonds of fellowship have been broken (and they are legion today!) to be regular in partaking of the Lord's Supper. I know of no other place where the trampled and hard-packed soil of a mistreated human heart can again be planted with the flowers of love and trust. When we consider the severe torment caused by ruptured fellowship among fellow employees, we can perhaps measure how many of our church members seek oil and balsam at the table of the Lord for the psychic mistreatment of the week and strengthen themselves anew to withstand the hundred small humiliations yet to come.

In this connection I am reminded of a special group of

communicants which probably every Swiss pastor has encountered in one form or another. These are persons who suffer not merely because of the break in the bonds of family fellowship but also because the bonds of fellowship between nations have been ruptured. Let us examine for a moment two such cases as representative of many thousands. One was a German; she was a German through and through and would never change. However, as a foreigner she felt such a debt of gratitude to her host country that it was impossible for her to become an active member of any Nazi organization in Switzerland. News of the events in her homeland under the Nazi regime drove her to the brink of melancholia. In the meantime, aversion and hate grew up in Switzerland against anyone who spoke German natively but with a non-Swiss accent. She knew the cause of this hate and understood its justification. Her pronounced North German accent immediately gave her away as a native of Germany; no one would think her a citizen of German-speaking Switzerland. And so she gradually became shy and unsociable and scarcely dared speak. Things finally went so far that she came to her pastor and in all seriousness asked him if she, as a German citizen, were still permitted to attend church services. Urgently she asked not to be excluded from the table of the Lord, despite the fact that she was a German. The table of the Lord had become a refuge for this poor person, her last and only refuge. For this soul who suffered to the point of collapse because she knew what was happening in her country and could not change it, the table of the Lord had become a real "asylum" and a place of shelter from the "poisonous arrows of Satan." The angels in heaven rejoice when the miracle of such communion takes place in the midst of war. But there where the invisible history of the world is being recorded, God alone knows the names of all those in all lands who in this way flee to the table of reconciliation bearing the burden of the ruptured fellowship among nations.

And then there was another person, a small Jew who trembled nervously after all the mistreatment he had suffered and fears he had withstood. For three years he had been regularly attending church services in some town or another in Switzerland and had been attending communicants' class. For a long time he had wanted to be baptized, but one consideration kept him from it: his lack of economic freedom and his financial dependence on a refugee organization. He was fearful lest others, and he himself, perhaps think that he wanted baptism for improper motives, even if unconsciously so. After quite a struggle he finally decided to postpone his baptism until the day of freedom, but in the meanwhile he longed for Christian fellowship. One day he made a strange request of the local pastor; he wanted permission to partake of the Lord's Supper even though he had not been baptized. And his request was granted. This was heresy, to be sure, and is certainly not to be recommended as a general course of action. However, in this one case, on the basis of prophetic freedom and responsibility, so to speak, participation in the Lord's Supper might become a sign of the great future and total fellowship for which we hope and long, but which now is still curbed and ruptured— a rupture which we must bear bravely.

We have now come to the boundary between the difficulties inherent in the Lord's Supper and those for which we men are responsible. We are not to bear those difficulties for which we are responsible, but rather are to struggle against them with all our strength. We shall speak of this in the next six sections of this essay.

The Neglect of the Lord's Supper

We usually think of the many people who no longer attend the Lord's Supper when we speak of the indifference and neglect shown this sacrament; however, these are not the only ones who may be reproached. From a Biblical point of view, it is primarily the participants who must be reproached, and especially those who stand *behind* the communion table—the pastors and the assisting elders of the church. Indeed, if we take the Holy Scripture as our standard, the whole official church today is guilty of neglecting the Lord's Supper. This neglect is revealed primarily by the frequency—or rather the infrequency—with which the Lord's Supper is celebrated. We know that originally it was celebrated not merely every Sunday, but on each day of the week as well. Yet in the Swiss church of today we have communion on the average of five times a year: Christmas, Good Friday, Easter, Whitsunday, and Rogation Day. However, this certainly does not mean that every church celebrates the Lord's Supper at least on these five occasions. On the contrary, the churches which have communion on these five days are the last remnant of the past. Perhaps some of the readers might know of a church in Switzerland which does not celebrate the Lord's Supper at all. This is certainly a possibility, although I myself do not know of any congregation which has dared take this final step. However, I do know of a congregation which approximately twenty years ago for a time had the Lord's Supper only once a year: on the one day on which they celebrated Rogation Day, Atonement Day, and Swiss Federation Day. Certainly it would not be at all surprising to find a church which followed this development to the final conclusion and completely stopped celebrating the Lord's Supper. In fact, it is not easy to see why pastors and church officials suddenly halted at the number five in this catastrophic waste of our heritage. If, for example, it seemed proper and advisable— for reasons which we cannot grasp—to remove the Lord's Supper from one of the five Biblical festive days, Ascension Day, why not eliminate it from one of the other feast days as well? (Incidentally, there has been some talk recently about the "Plight of Ascension Day," because the Lord's Supper has been dropped from the celebration of this of all days.)

In any event, our congregations must give grave and serious thought toward conquering this difficulty. Certainly we do not mean to say that the problem of neglect will be eliminated if the church leaders order more frequent celebration of the Lord's Supper. On the other hand, we must seriously consider what Eduard Thurneysen says in his interpretation of Paul's letter to the Philippians: "Everything alive which is entrusted to us, be it flower or child, needs care that it may grow and flourish. Things are destroyed so quickly! And that which is divine is the most alive of anything that can be given us. Therefore, people who have begun to perceive the divine must be given this admonition: Take care that the divine remains alive." This admonition to do something which basically is quite obvious, that is, to care for what has been given to us alive, is particularly applicable to the celebration of the Lord's Supper in the local church. We can hardly say that we have "taken care." If we had, the celebration of the Lord's Supper would not have been reduced to five times a year.

Some years ago the pastor of one of our churches received a visit from a Christian woman who was eighty years old and who had succeeded in remaining "alive." She expressed her longing to go to the table of the Lord each Sunday after the sermon along with the other members of the church. The idea seemed strange and foreign to the pastor, as it may seem to some readers of this essay. Today, however, the congregation celebrates communion once a month, that is, approximately fourteen times a year. At first, the officers of the church expressed fear that more frequent celebration would reduce attendance, and certainly there would be some grounds for concern. However, in this case the very opposite was true. Attendance at the Lord's Supper increased through the introduction of these so-called "Extra Communion Services."

Whether the church will ever again reach the point of issuing the invitation to the table of the Lord every Sunday must of course not be merely a question of an organizational nature—let that once again be emphasized. It is not true that increasing the number of celebrations of the Lord's Supper can free us from our negligence. However, the converse is true—conquering this difficulty will be a fruit of new thinking on the essence and nature of the sacraments and will depend on the extent to which the Christian church is awake and alive.

The Agape

The agape (the love feast in which the congregation participates as a whole) has all but disappeared from the church of today—a fact which is closely connected with the problem discussed in the preceding section. We might add that an awakening of the church will lead not only to painstaking care of the Lord's Supper but will also soon lead to a return of the agape. However, we must be careful not to cling fearfully to any concept of one particular form of the love feast. Each period in history will give new forms of fellowship in the agape, if the church keeps abreast of the times.

Some churches today do have events somewhat resembling the agape, even if they do not have real agapes. In Basel, for example, the elderly members of every church meet once a month for coffee and cake. One congregation traditionally meets twice a year to eat and drink together as a congregation, once in the fall at Thanksgiving and once in the early summer during cherry time. The whole congregation walks out to a farm on the outskirts of the town and there on the meadow has tea and bread together, giving thanks to God for the fruitfulness of the land. There are many opportunities for the young people of the congregation to eat together and be under the same roof. For example, every member brings something to a common tea, or supper, or Christmas party, and all the food is pooled. Something of this real fellowship takes place in youth hostels during weekends, and on school vacations and field trips. I also recall several weddings and baptisms at which a majority of the congregation was present but which by no means degenerated into revelry; in their spirit these occasions were more like agapes.

Here we must sound the warning against anything that is merely of an organizational nature. Nonetheless, unsuspected possibilities in the life of the church will open up to a congregation whenever a breath of that spirit begins to blow which is described in Acts: "And all who believed were together and had all things in common; and they sold their possessions and goods and distributed them to all, as any had need." (Acts 2:44-45.) If an increase in such agape-like occasions should finally lead to a return of the true agape—and this is what we should expect in a Christian congregation—we must be careful to see to it that the love feast is the fruit of the growing blessing of the fellowship of the Lord's Supper. This does not mean that the love feast and the Lord's Supper must take place at the same time and place. However, any agape-like fellowship developed within the framework of the church must finally and consciously be rooted in the community of the Lord's Supper if it is not to degenerate and become empty; it must draw its substance and force from this source. In our present day, however, we can do no more than speak of those practices which show some signs of the agape; and as a rule even these practices are scarcely more than matters of chance or local custom.

An increase in the spirit of the agape—which we should hope and pray for—will yield an energetic expansion of service within the local church. Indeed, we cannot doubt that such a development will result in strengthening and renewing fellowship in the home, the family, at work, and in the nation as a whole. The position of the old person in society will become an acute problem in the next few decades when couples with few or no children reach old age.

The church will not do its duty merely by rejecting and combating as a matter of principle any proposal to kill these "useless lives." It also will not be enough for the state to establish comfortable old folks' homes—or even palaces— in the form of model farms. Only the spirit of the Biblical love feast will give the lonely old person his seat at the table of men, due him in accordance with the will of God. The fact that man does not live by bread alone, but rather from each single word which comes from the mouth of God, is particularly true of the aged.

Administering the Lord's Supper to the Sick

In this section we shall consider the sick and infirm who are physically unable to come to the table of the Lord in the church sanctuary. In administering the Lord's Supper to such people we must keep three main points in mind.

In the first place, the sick are not served with the Sacrament alone. They must first be served with the Word and must also be brought into the fellowship of those who hear the proclamation of the Word; that is, they must be visited regularly, either by the pastor or by members of the congregation. Every Sunday they should receive a message, either printed or read aloud; if possible, this message should be delivered in person rather than by mail. It is good if the congregation can distribute to the sick and infirm a copy of the same sermon delivered at the church service. And when we consider fellowship in the Word, we must also realize that fellowship in prayer is closely allied; the Lord's Supper cannot be administered to the sick without the fellowship of prayer coming as a result. We must rediscover the mys-

teries which exist between the congregation of active communicants and the sick and infirm.

In the second place, we must see to it that if possible the
sick partake of the sacraments on the same day the Lord's
Supper is celebrated by the congregation. First of all, it
often reduces the feeling of isolation if the minister can tell
the sick person that he is partaking of the same bread, from
the same loaf, as did the congregation. This also keeps the
sick from having the depressing feeling that he has caused
the congregation extra trouble. And finally it avoids raising
the fatal thought in the mind of the sick person that his condition must be critical, since the sacraments are "already"
being brought him. We must do anything to avoid giving
the impression of "extreme unction."

In the third place, we should see to it that one or more
people partake of the sacraments along with the sick person.
If this is not possible, the minister himself should commune.

I might mention a special and unusual difficulty in administering the sacraments at one particular sickbed. A hospital patient whose home was in another country wanted to
take communion. He knew that his days were numbered,
but he wanted to wait until his wife and grown children
could be present and go to the table of the Lord with him.
By the time they had arrived, however, his condition had
worsened to the extent that it was physically impossible for
him to eat and drink. What could be done? At the advice
of an experienced minister who was consulted, the patient
did manage to partake of the sacraments with his family
in the following way. He took the bread and cup into his
hand, looked at them, put them to his lips symbolically and
then handed them back to the minister. Let this unusual
case serve to illustrate that we are free from all legalistic

formalism in the sacraments. Especially in administering the Lord's Supper to the sick and dying we are faced time and time again with unforeseen situations where love must act free from all anxious ritualism.

In this connection I should like to point to a scene described in *The Fishermen of the Lofooten Islands,* a novel by the Scandinavian author Johann Bojer. At one point in the story, the men are celebrating the Lord's Supper with a dying comrade who had requested communion. They are doing this without pastor and without liturgy. "They had no wine and also no proper bread, but there was no time for long deliberation. The candle-end in the bottle was burning, and all sat in silence as Hendrick went to his chest and pulled out a small bottle of Riga balm. He poured a little into a coffee cup, mixed in some water and tasted it. Then he cut off a piece of his fine cake which he put on a tin plate. With the plate and cup in his hand he went up to the dying man, knelt and set them on the floor. . . ." If it was possible in Biblical times to baptize with stagnant water instead of with flowing water and further if it was possible to break fish instead of bread, should it not also be possible, if necessary, to drink another liquid at the Lord's Supper in place of wine?

Consideration of the Weak

We now come to a problem which we must not minimize by saying that it concerns only individual cases who do not need to be considered when measured against the great majority of the congregation. We must discuss the special problem of drinkers and total abstainers. If it is true that as one member suffers so all members suffer, then we must take these special cases seriously—particularly since the problem involves weak members of the congregation.

There are two sides to this problem. The first involves young people who are taking communion for the first time and who, from their childhood on, have been told that alcohol is the poison of all poisons and the horror of all horrors. Either through propagandistic influence or, more frequently, through painful experiences in their immediate families they have been abstainers since early childhood and now for the first time in their lives they are to drink alcohol —at communion, of all places. This is a problem which we must not overlook.

And then there is the other side of the problem: former drinkers who have pledged to abstain. To be sure, the oath of abstinence does allow participation in the Lord's Supper, but it is a fact that a former drinker can be led into temptation by drinking communion wine. Anyone familiar with the nature of addiction will immediately see that fear of a relapse is neither unfounded nor exaggerated. The habitual smoker, for example, can feel a violent urge to smoke when he sees an actor light a cigarette in a moving picture. The alcoholic can even fall if he catches the scent of wine coming from the ventilator of a tavern which he might chance to pass. At the communion table the scent more than the taste of alcoholic wine can lead the weak into temptation. We must take this fact into account. However, it is of great importance that the change from alcoholic to nonalcoholic communion wine be done properly and be based on the evangel. Two examples may serve to illustrate what is meant.

A certain teacher, an abstainer and a zealous leader of a local charity organization, felt conscience-bound to petition the officers of her church to eliminate alcoholic communion wine. The reason given was that abstinence should be practiced not only by all Christians but also by all thinking and decent people. Her fight was well meant but was not waged with the proper weapon. As a result of her legalistic reasoning the petition was not granted—and with a certain justification, since it was not based on the evangel.

On the other hand, a similar petition was made to the officers of another Swiss church. This petition, however, was submitted for the proper reasons—a request that brotherly consideration be taken of the weak members of the congregation—and was not based on a demand for universal abstinence. At first the petition was denied because the pastor, formerly an abstainer, allowed himself to be carried away in a meeting with the officers and stated that the soundness and thus the validity of the Lord's Supper depended on having alcoholic communion wine. Since a unanimous decision could not be reached, the petitioners had the wisdom to withdraw their petition quietly. But several years later, after the death of the minister who had opposed the petition, alcoholic communion wine was replaced by nonalcoholic wine one Thursday of Holy Week, by unanimous vote of the officers. Their decision, reached after careful deliberation, was made only on the basis of brotherly consideration and was independent of the question of abstinence. The congregation was not informed of the change in advance, and the reaction was as slight as if a different table cloth, or communion cup, or bread tray had been used. For the most part the congregation did not even notice, and those who did silently accepted the change—slight to be sure, but yet not unimportant for certain individual members.

Preparation for the Lord's Supper

There are two more problems which the local congregation must overcome correctly, that is, in an evangelical manner: preparation for the Lord's Supper, and the so-called discipline of the Lord's Supper. We shall discuss these two problems in this section and the next.

In his work mentioned above, Oscar Cullmann demonstrates convincingly that the basic elements of every early Christian worship service were a combination of preaching, prayer, and the Lord's Supper. Preaching without Holy Communion or Holy Communion without preaching was not customary. Preaching and the Lord's Supper cannot be separated because, as we tried to show in the first part of our discussion, the Lord's Supper is unthinkable without faith, and faith comes from preaching. There is also a practical reason for the inseparability of Word and sacrament, in addition to the historical and doctrinal reasons just mentioned: The Word prepares the congregation to take communion. Auricular confession is the preparation for Roman Catholic communion, while preparation for the evangelical Lord's Supper consists of hearing the Word—that is, the individual and the congregation encounter the Bible. The evangelical proclamation of the Word is properly not the preaching of morals, but rather the presentation of the gospel and the message of joy and of grace, and is thus encouragement and preparation for communion. Under the sovereign action of the Holy Spirit, "binding and loosing" takes place through this expression of the word of grace.

Needless to say, individual ministry is not excluded; preaching brings about ministering conversation in private. Personal discussions can be of additional help in preparing persons for the Lord's Supper, but ministry to the individual in private is not a necessary prerequisite to Holy Communion. The sermon normally gives real and wholly sufficient preparation for the Lord's Supper. It is during the sermon that consciences are examined in the sense of Psalm 139 through the free act of the Holy Spirit, and here it is that the miracle of repentance takes place. The gentle, and at the same time powerful, grip of the Word makes us ready to forgive as we ourselves are forgiven. And, even more than that, the Word can move the hearer to go to the brother who has something against him; it can also cause one brother to confess his sins to another and talk with him. Indeed, by means of the Word the Holy Spirit can cause a member of the congregation to seek out his pastor, or perhaps a believing family physician or neighbor or grandmother. It may be useful—in fact, it is even desirable—if there can be ministering conversation before the taking of communion, whether it be in private or in the presence of two or three witnesses. We even welcome the fact that such ministering is given in abundance, but there is no room for legal compulsion to private discussion within the evangelical church, nor can we think of such discussions as an indispensable prerequisite to the Lord's Supper. The following letter, written by a woman no longer among us, may show how the sermon usually prepares the congregation for the Lord's Supper:

"I had made up my mind to go to the table of the Lord

on Sunday. But Sunday morning I did not feel properly prepared and said to myself that I could not, or rather should not, take communion with this feeling. However, in the sermon I heard the great words that we are permitted to go to the table of the Lord laden with sin and guilt if we go with the sincere petition that Christ remove and forgive our sins. Then I heard two voices within me. One encouraged me: 'Stay and go to the Lord's table'; the other said, 'Leave this place.' The second voice almost won, for after the benediction I got up and started for the door. Still, the first voice again urged me to say and take communion. I had to sit down again.

"What I was permitted to experience after the communion service was the work of God, not of man, and I know that it was the voice of God that had invited me to remain. Many years ago I worked in a store along with another woman in our church. At that time she was still unmarried. We had a falling out because of business matters. The first few years after our break we saw each other rarely. Since this church has been formed, however, we have rather frequently met at church and at the Bible hour, and I must confess that each time it has been quite unpleasant for me to meet her at such a place. It was not that I hated her or bore a grudge, but I did still suffer from the dissension between us, and if possible we still avoided each other. Last Sunday this woman also went to the Lord's table. But as she left the church she came up to me, offered me her hand, and said: 'Miss X, let's forgive and forget, shall we?' I cannot describe to you my joy. I was unable to speak. On the way home I thanked God."

Thus it is that the Holy Spirit wants to open up the way to the throne of grace through preaching. Whenever that great call is issued to the congregation on communion Sundays, "Come, for all is ready," a struggle arises in many a soul: "Shall I rise or remain seated?" The moment at which the benediction is said to the members who are leaving is so full of decision that the shepherd and the flock can only spend it in priestly supplication.

Discipline over the Lord's Supper

By "discipline over the Lord's Supper" we mean forbidding a church member to come to the communion table and refusing him the bread and the cup if he should present himself nonetheless. We reject this direct form of discipline as being unevangelical.

Nearly twenty years ago, when there was scarcely any youth work in the church, a rural congregation had a small and struggling boys' club which was often under attack. One of the worst boys in the village was among the few members; he was a well-known and feared rowdy who had taken it into his head to join the club—for reasons known only to himself. This was a heavy burden for the group to bear, particularly since the organization was under attack anyway, but the members stood it for more than two years. One morning after a club meeting the evening before, the whole town heard the news that on the preceding night two members of this pious group had wallowed on a manure pile after leaving the church and had "tried to ruin each other." After the matter had been handled in accordance with Matthew 18:15-17 and the behavior of the ruffian had still not changed, the decision was made, although with misgivings, to exclude him from the group. Communion Sunday came several weeks after this action, and the boy in question came to the table of the Lord. Were bread and the cup to be denied him? Was he to be turned away from that very table which is called the "table of the Lord"? He was given communion. That is in accordance with the evangel; room was also made at the father's table for the prodigal son. The communion table is a place which church government is not to touch. The Lord's table is the sanctuary of those who are excluded from all else. The Lord of the communion table bears those whom the church group can no longer bear, even with the best will. Church discipline must not extend to the Lord's Supper. The pastor may send a boy away, his comrades may no longer be able to stand him, but: "My father and my mother have forsaken me, but the LORD will take me up." (Psalm 27:10.)

And yet there is a form of discipline over the Lord's Supper in the evangelical church. It is of an indirect nature and comes into play indirectly through the sermon. The Word of God not only opens the way to the throne of grace, it can also close it; it can loose *and* bind, it can forgive *and* retain. A passage from the fourth chapter of Hebrews is applicable here in a special way: "For the word of God is living and active, sharper than any two-edged sword, piercing to the division of soul and spirit, of joints and marrow, and discerning the thoughts and intentions of the heart." (Hebrews 4:12.) The Word of God directed to the whole church is the "key of the kingdom" which was entrusted to Peter and thus to the church. Through the workings of the Holy Spirit the preaching which precedes the Lord's Supper is an opening and a closing. During the sermon the worshipers decide whether or not to remain for communion. Through preaching, the Holy Spirit can move us to come to the table of the Lord or to depart. In this way there is an indirect discipline over the Lord's Supper every communion Sunday, but it is a discipline which we humans sense more than control. The Word and Spirit of God is a good searcher of men's souls and is in addition a just and merciful disciplinarian.

At this point, however, we must note that another disciplinarian, an invisible one, is present, aside from the Holy Spirit: "the accuser . . . who accuses them day and night." (Revelation 12:10.) The attack is launched whenever the invitation to the Lord's table is given. In my own experience there are three main passages from the Bible which the accuser uses to assail the children of the Kingdom. The first is the phrase "visiting the iniquity of the fathers upon the children to the third and the fourth generation." (Exodus 20:5.) The second is the statement, "blasphemy against the Spirit will not be forgiven." (Matthew 12:31.) And finally we read of the communicant who "eats the bread or drinks the cup of the Lord in an unworthy manner," and "eats and drinks judgment upon himself." (1 Corinthians 11:27, 29.) The accuser most frequently uses this statement of unworthy participation in the Lord's Supper as a weapon in his struggle against attendance at communion. It is no rarity to see a timorous, indeed, despondent communicant who, "standing far off, would not even lift up his eyes to heaven." (Luke 18:13.) For the sake of this timid communicant it is necessary that a direct discipline through individual ministering stand open, quite aside from the discipline of the sermon. This direct discipline may consist in counseling a church member who comes to us and asks in doubt whether he may take communion; in rare cases our advice may be for him not to come to the Lord's table this one time. But such direct discipline must never be more than fatherly and brotherly advice. In the overwhelming majority of cases, however, the task of the ministrant will be the very opposite; it will be to talk with the tired, encourage the despondent, lift up those who have been struck down, and blow on the embers that they may burn again.

In addition to this ministering advice we should also consider the prophetic threat, which borders on direct discipline. Our attention is, of course, immediately directed to 1 Corinthians 5. The congregation can be told of the punishment and threat applicable to offenders against the Lord's Supper, but in the final analysis the question of the offender is a matter for the Holy Spirit. When we read, "Let not many of you become teachers" (James 3:1), how much less shall we undertake to be prophets?

Thus there remains the evangelical rule that preaching exercises indirect discipline over the Lord's Supper through the Holy Spirit. However, direct exclusion from the Lord's Supper, excommunication, is not in accordance with the evangel. In every evangelical congregation there is a register of those who are invited and entitled to communion: the church roll. Sometimes we may be dangerously tempted to take the roll of communicants more firmly in hand and subject it to critical examination, that is, to admit to the Lord's Supper only those who fulfill certain conditions. This is the temptation to exercise direct discipline over the Lord's Supper. If we should succumb to this temptation, however, there would be real danger of the ecclesiastical authority of our offices becoming positions of arrogated power. This is a danger with which we are only too well acquainted. From that very moment on, we would no longer be servants of salvation, we would be masters.

If we go beyond indirect discipline in our ministering advice or prophetic threat, we must be very much on guard that direct discipline does not become "judging before the time." Two parables of our Lord impose strict limitations on evangelical church discipline. The first is the parable of the weeds among the wheat; not until later was the field cleared of weeds. The other is the parable of the great net which was drawn to the shore so that the good fish could be separated from the bad. In these parables the clearing out of the weeds and the sorting of the fish was not the work of men; it was the work of the angelic servants. Not until the last, the great Lord's Supper of the nations, will there be the call, "Force them to come in," and only at that time and place will the guest who is not in wedding attire be ordered from the table. For this reason we give the adult members of the church permanent permission to participate in the Lord's Supper after they have been properly instructed. We do not take hold of the "keys of the kingdom" more firmly than this. It is not up to us to determine when and to what extent the church member makes use of this permission which has been granted him once and for all. We may leave that to Him who alone knows the hearts of men and who has commissioned His church "to preach the gospel to the whole creation." And we may then leave it to the Holy Spirit to determine what He wants to do through this Word which opens or closes the door.

Three Incidental Observations

Three short remarks should be made before this essay is concluded. First: Of all the problems surrounding the Lord's Supper, we have not mentioned the greatest one for which we men are responsible. A thorough examination of this problem would burst the very binding of this slender volume, but we should at least mention the point in passing. Because there is no Lord's Supper without preaching and no sacrament without the Word, there is consequently no problem surrounding the Lord's Supper which is not concurrently and decisively a problem in which preaching is involved. In the evangelical church the *plight of preaching* is the most consequential of all the problems associated with the Lord's Supper. We have already seen that the faith which is necessary at the Lord's Supper comes from preaching. But what if faith does *not* come from preaching? And what if preaching even produces active, aggressive *unbelief?* In the Bible unbelief is never represented as an unalterable fate, but rather as an offense. What can be done? Let us quickly glance at what is involved. A struggle between faith and unbelief is raging within the church, and on no account are we to avoid this struggle. However, we must not quarrel or fight for power; rather we are to wage our struggle with the weapons of the Spirit which the Lord of the church has entrusted to us: repentance, prayer, and indefatigable preaching of faith.

Second: What do we do with different or even conflicting preaching about the possibility of a common celebration of the Lord's Supper? It seems to us that there are two narrow paths available which can both be trod in truthfulness and in brotherly love. Either: We recognize the differences and are aware of them—indeed, we work out these differences in spiritual wrestling—and then go to a common celebration of the Lord's Supper, *despite* the differences which exist. This fellowship in the Lord's Supper is then a "nonetheless" of *faith*. Or: In such circumstances we renounce a common celebration of the Lord's Supper, in which case our renunciation is to be borne as spiritual fasting. This second course, the course chosen by Luther and Zwingli, is no less a way of love than the first. Just as the first way emphasizes love without betraying truth, so the second underscores truth without sacrificing love. A third way, however, which is unfortunately the most popular by far, would seem to us to be reprehensible above all: "Acting as if." The differences are bridged romantically, are minimized or even consciously concealed, and there is a common celebration of the Lord's Supper for the sake of sweet peace and the preservation of appearances to the outside world. This third way serves neither truth nor love; it is a broad road and leads to ruin.

Third: When we look back over the terrain which we have traversed together, we are joyfully and gratefully astonished that the Lord's Supper exists in our evangelical church. In any case, it will be hard for us to find a historical reason or any other rational explanation for the fact that the Lord's Supper actually does exist at all in the evangelical church and that it is celebrated from time to time by congregations in our land. We owe this astonishing circumstance not to human merit but to the favor of Him who quite obviously wishes to maintain what He has established. Something of what the Lord of the Lord's Supper has promised for His whole church has been fulfilled before the eyes of all with the Lord's Supper: The gates of hell were not able to prevail against the evangelical Lord's Supper. To be sure, we men have often enough had bad intentions with this sacrament, but God's intentions have been good. This is the reason that we have been in the fortunate position of thinking about "The Lord's Supper in the Local Congregation"—a position which we should not take as a matter of course. However, the fact that the Lord's Supper which was founded by the Lord still exists today and that it will be given to evangelical Christendom tomorrow in new and deeper understanding towers brightly above everything that we have said here about the existence of the Lord's Supper in the local church—a sacrament full of problems, but yet so full of promise. The meal in the pot and the oil in the jar have not run out, and despite the famine in the land there goes out into this world the great call to that table which "is prepared in the presence of all enemies."